The Political Economy of Development

Those studying development often address the impact of government policies, but rarely the politics that generate these policies. A culmination of several decades of work by Robert Bates, among the most respected comparativists in political science, this compact volume seeks to rectify that omission. Bates addresses the political origins of prosperity and security and uncovers the root causes of under-development. Without the state there can be no development, but those who are endowed with the power of the state often use its power to appropriate the wealth and property of those they rule. When do those with power use it to safeguard rather than to despoil? Bates explores this question by analyzing motivations behind the behavior of governments in the developing world, drawing on historical and anthropological insights, game theory, and his own field research in developing nations.

Robert H. Bates, Eaton Professor Emeritus of the Science of Government at Harvard University, is the author, co-author, or editor of over a dozen books on the developing world. He specializes on the study of conflict and Africa, where he has spent much of his research career. A member of the American Academy of Arts and Sciences and National Academy of Sciences, he has held professorships at the California Institute of Technology, Duke University and the Toulouse School of Economics.

CAMBRIDGE STUDIES IN COMPARATIVE POLITICS

GENERAL EDITORS

KATHLEEN THELEN *Massachusetts Institute of Technology*

ASSOCIATE EDITORS

CATHERINE BOONE *London School of Economics*
THAD DUNNING *University of California, Berkeley*
ANNA GRZYMALA-BUSSE *Stanford University*
TORBEN IVERSEN *Harvard University*
STATHIS KALYVAS *University of Oxford*
MARGARET LEVI *Stanford University*
MELANIE MANION *Duke University*
HELEN MILNER *Princeton University*
FRANCES ROSENBLUTH *Yale University*
SUSAN STOKES *Yale University*
TARIQ THACHIL *University of Pennsylvania*
ERIK WIBBELS *Duke University*

SERIES FOUNDER

Peter Lange *Duke University*

OTHER BOOKS IN THE SERIES

Christopher Adolph, *Bankers, Bureaucrats, and Central Bank Politics: The Myth of Neutrality*
Michael Albertus, *Autocracy and Redistribution: The Politics of Land Reform*
Michael Albertus *Property Without Rights: Origins and Consequences of the Property Rights Gap*
Santiago Anria, *When Movements Become Parties: The Bolivian MAS in Comparative Perspective*
Ben W. Ansell, *From the Ballot to the Blackboard: The Redistributive Political Economy of Education*
Ben W. Ansell and Johannes Lindvall, *Inward Conquest: The Political Origins of Modern Public Services*
Ben W. Ansell and David J. Samuels, *Inequality and Democratization: An Elite-Competition Approach*
Adam Michael Auerbach, *Demanding Development: The Politics of Public Goods Provision in India's Urban Slums*
Ana Arjona, *Rebelocracy: Social Order in the Colombian Civil War*
Leonardo R. Arriola, *Multi-Ethnic Coalitions in Africa: Business Financing of Opposition Election Campaigns*

Continued after the index

The Political Economy of Development

A Game Theoretic Approach

ROBERT H. BATES

Harvard University

CAMBRIDGE
UNIVERSITY PRESS

CAMBRIDGE
UNIVERSITY PRESS

University Printing House, Cambridge CB2 8BS, United Kingdom

One Liberty Plaza, 20th Floor, New York, NY 10006, USA

477 Williamstown Road, Port Melbourne, VIC 3207, Australia

314–321, 3rd Floor, Plot 3, Splendor Forum, Jasola District Centre, New Delhi – 110025, India

79 Anson Road, #06–04/06, Singapore 079906

Cambridge University Press is part of the University of Cambridge.

It furthers the University's mission by disseminating knowledge in the pursuit of education, learning, and research at the highest international levels of excellence.

www.cambridge.org
Information on this title: www.cambridge.org/9781108837507
DOI: 10.1017/9781108946315

© Robert H. Bates 2021

First published 2021

A catalogue record for this publication is available from the British Library.

Library of Congress Cataloging-in-Publication Data
NAMES: Bates, Robert H., author.
TITLE: The political economy of development : a game theoretic approach / Robert H. Bates, Harvard University, Massachusetts.
DESCRIPTION: Cambridge, United Kingdom ; New York, NY : Cambridge University Press, 2021. | Series: Cambridge studies in comparative politics | Includes index.
IDENTIFIERS: LCCN 2020039303 (print) | LCCN 2020039304 (ebook) | ISBN 9781108837507 (hardback) | ISBN 9781108946315 (ebook)
SUBJECTS: LCSH: Economic development. | Human services.
CLASSIFICATION: LCC HD75 .B379 2021 (print) | LCC HD75 (ebook) | DDC 338.9–dc23
LC record available at https://lccn.loc.gov/2020039303
LC ebook record available at https://lccn.loc.gov/2020039304

ISBN 978-1-108-83750-7 Hardback
ISBN 978-1-108-93093-2 Paperback

I dedicate this book to those who have inspired and instructed me: the coauthors of the papers woven into this volume.

Jean Paul Azam

Bruno Biais

David Epstein

Avner Greif

Da-Hsiang Donald Lien

William Rogerson

Smita Singh

David Soskice

I dedicate it as well to my students and colleagues at the California Institute of Technology, Duke University, and Harvard.

Contents

Figures

A Note to the Reader

The chapters in this book first appeared as articles. Each was written in response to an issue that arose while thinking about the role of politics in development. When I believed that I had thought things through, I then discussed my ideas with colleagues – many of whom were far more mathematically skilled than I – seeking to see if my arguments were persuasive and their logic valid. These discussions resulted in a series of coauthored papers, each analytic and based on formal arguments, which I have gathered and redrafted for inclusion in this book.

Though the papers are coauthored, I write here in the first person. In effect, I have recrafted and "repurposed" these earlier writings for I have themes I wish to advance and arguments I wish to explore and I draw upon these papers to do so. The arguments advanced in these chapters are therefore "on me" and the coauthors of the original papers are not to be held accountable for their shortcomings.

I

Introduction

Throughout this book, "development" refers to two things, the one economic and the other political. The first is prosperity, or the level of per capita income. The second is security, or the degree of safety of life and property. Nations that are prosperous have undergone a "great transformation," to adopt Polanyi's phrase.[1] Once based on agriculture, their economies are now industrial and their people live in cities rather than in villages or on farms. In most, people have ceded control over the means of violence from private to public hands. Insofar as the word "development" refers to the rise of prosperity and the attainment of security, then, it refers to the growth and transformation of the economy and to the rise of the state.

Those who study development glean their data from two major sources. The first is history: they gain insight into the process of development by comparing the economies and polities of today's advanced industrial nations with the economies and polities that they possessed in the past.[2] The second is the contemporary world. By comparing the advanced industrial nations with those whose economies remain agrarian and poor, researchers probe the process

---

[1] Karl Polanyi, 1957, *The Great Transformation*. Boston: Beacon Press.
[2] See, for example, Daron Acemoglu and James Robinson, 2019, *The Narrow Corridor*. New York: The Beacon Press; Carles Boix, 2015, *Political Order and Inequality*. New York: Cambridge University Press; Frances Fukuyama, 2011, *The Origins of Political Order*. New York: Farrar, Stevens, and Giroux; and Margaret Levi, 1989, *Of Rule and Revenue*. Berkeley and Los Angeles: University of California Press.

of development. Economic historians stand among the most energetic
and productive of those who pursue the first strategy; anthropologists,
development economists, and political scientists number among those
who most actively pursue the second. In this volume, I draw on both.
And in doing so, I make use of the theory of games.

In the contemporary period, when social scientists turn to the study
of development, most make use of quantitative data. They seek to
extract valid inferences by randomizing their observations and introduc-
ing case controls.[3] Here I approach the study of development in
a different fashion. Rather than assembling quantitative data sets,
I draw upon narrative accounts. In doing so, I extract insights from
these histories by applying formal theory and, in particular, the theory
of games.

Game theory enables us to transform qualitative data – reports, histories, or narratives – into causal explanations. To do so, the analyst first
identifies the actors, the constraints they face, the alternatives available to
them, the responses they anticipate, and the payoffs that then accrue.
Assuming them to be rational, the analyst then identifies the strategies
that the actors are likely to pursue. And if her "theory of the case" is
correct, the outcome she observes should correspond to what she has
anticipated when analyzing the game.

Proceeding in this fashion, I first journey to South Sudan and address
Evans-Pritchard's classic study of the Nuer. In chapter 2 we learn that the
price of peace is insecurity; in societies without states, peace exists in the
shadow of the feud. Turning to Chapter 3, we learn that the relationship
holds more broadly: in societies without states, we find, development
cannot be attained: one can have either prosperity or security, but not
both. In Chapter 4, I set out the conditions under which states can form,
thus making it possible to prosper while remaining secure. It is the formation of states, we argue, that makes it possible to develop.

While the presence of a state may fulfill a necessary condition for
development, however, it surely cannot be sufficient, for history has
shown that those who control the state can use its power to seize the
wealth of others. Recognizing that this is the case, Chapters 5 and 6
explore how states can be rendered "developmental."

Up to this point, the chapters have found focused on the politics
of development and the problem of security. Chapter 7 focuses

---

[3] Most notably, of course, my Cambridge colleagues, Michael Kremer Abhijt Banarjee and
Ester Duflo – winners of the 2019 Nobel Prize in economics.

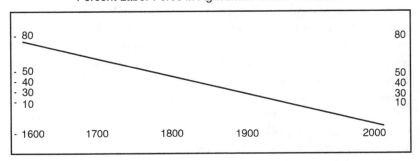

FIGURE I.I Data: Percent of labor force in agriculture in OECD countries, over time

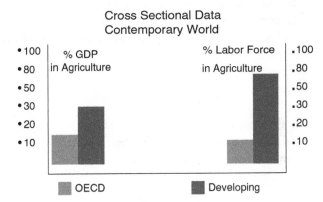

FIGURE I.2 Cross-sectional data on the contemporary world

instead on the economics of development and the possibility of prosperity. Having undergone the great transformation, industry's share of the national product has increased and the share of agriculture declined (Figures I.I and I.2).

To account for this transformation, scholars – both Marxist and neo-classical – tend to treat economic "sectors" as if they were political actors and to attribute development to the political power of industrial capital and to the declining importance of agriculture.[4] And yet the historical record reveals that before the great transformation, when agriculture dominated the national economy, many governments strove to promote the fortunes of industry; thus the mercantilist policies they adopted in Early Modern Europe.[5] It also reveals that when industry at last became the dominant sector, many governments then championed the fortunes of agriculture; governments in the advanced industrial nations commonly subsidize the incomes of farmers.[6] The obvious disjuncture between the economic significance and the political prominence of sectors of the economy leads us to seek an alternative way of explaining the "great transformation." In Chapter 7, I offer one: an approach based on interest groups rather than sectors – an approach that generates the paradoxical outcomes that we observe.

Chapter 8 draws together what we have learned about the impact of politics upon the economics of development. Deploying the standard Lewis model,[7] it illustrates how varying degrees of political insecurity can generate the growth paths traced by many developing economies. Doing so, it limns the political foundations of economic development.

A NOTE ON METHODS

To reiterate: throughout this volume, I instead use formal theory, drawing principally on the theory of games.[8] Game-theoretic models enable us to make systematic use of qualitative data and to generate

---

[4] Be they Marxist (Steven Marcus, 2015, *Engels, Manchester, and the Working Class*. Piscataway, NJ: Transaction Publishers), or neo-classical (Deepak Lal, 1985, *The Poverty of Development Economics*. Cambridge, MA: Harvard University Press).

[5] Thus the literature on mercantilism. See, for example, Eli Heckscher, 1955, *Mercantilism*, 2 vols. Trans. Mendel Shapiro. London: George Allen and Unwin.

[6] As by promoting agricultural exports, limiting agricultural imports, stockpiling agricultural surpluses. See, for example, Grant McConnell, 1966, *Private Power and American Democracy*. New York: Knopf.

[7] A. Lewis, 1954, "Economic Development with Unlimited Supplies of Labor." *Manchester School of Economic and Social Studies* 22, 139–191.

[8] To emphasize yet again: When I write "I," I am referring not only to myself but also to my coauthors.

explanations for the political outcomes we observe.[9] Being formal, once depicted as a game, these accounts yield conclusions that *must* follow. They can therefore be tested. The use of game theory thus enables us to make systematic use of qualitative data and to do so in a rigorous manner.

[9] See Robert H. Bates, Avner Greif, Margaret Levi, Jean-Laureant Rosenthal, and Barry Weingast, 1998, *Analytic Narratives*. Princeton: Princeton University Press.

2

Societies without States

These affairs are like a game in which everybody knows the rules and states of development: when one is expected to give way, when to be firm, when to yield at the last moment, and so forth.[1]

We begin with a reanalysis of Evans-Pritchard's classic account of the Nuer: a stateless society. Among the Nuer, kin groups govern, he noted, and the means of violence therefore remained in private hands. How then could there be order? We recast his answer using elementary game theory.[2] Doing so not only leads us to a clearer understanding of his analysis, but also to a deeper understanding of the Nuer's political system – and of the advantages of the state.

Among the Nuer, the polity consists of families and kin. While lacking a bureaucracy, a judiciary or a police force, Evans-Pritchard notes, peace nonetheless prevails. Should one person harm another, the victim's family seeks revenge; knowing that they will do so, he observes, people then refrain from attacking others. Rather than a state, it is thus the family that guarantees security. In the phrasing of Max Gluckman, Evans-Pritchard demonstrates that among the Nuer, peace lies in "the shadow of the feud."[3] It is insecurity – the threat of reprisals by kin – that preserves the peace.

Adapted from Robert Bates, 1983, "The Preservation of Order in Stateless Societies: A Re-interpretation of Evan-Pritchard's *The Nuer*," in *Essays on the Political Economy of Rural Africa*. Berkeley and Los Angeles: University of California Press, pp. 7–20. Transforming the original article into a chapter for a book led to the rewriting of portions of the text. In no way do these alterations affect the arguments originally advanced.
[1] E. E. Evans-Pritchard, 1940, *The Nuer*. Oxford: The Clarendon Press, pp. 175–176.
[2] Ibid.   [3] Max Gluckman, 1955, *Custom and Conflict in Africa*. Oxford: Blackwell.

In this chapter, I explore Evans-Pritchard's account of how order can be preserved in the absence of a state and the limitations of this system of government.

THE SETTING

The Nuer are a pastoralist people. While they do cultivate gardens, they principally engage in rearing cattle. As Evans-Pritchard puts it, the Nuer "not only depend on cattle for many of life's necessities but they have the herdsman's outlook on the world. Cattle are their dearest possession."[4] Cattle are the main property among the Nuer, and the joint family – the father, his sons, and their wives – is the elementary property-holding unit. Each family seeks to care for, nurture, and increase its cattle holdings. Evans-Pritchard reports that they expend great effort in this endeavor and succeed remarkably well.[5]

Among the Nuer, breeding and raising cattle provides one means of increasing one's property. Another means, at least in theory, is theft. Each property owner could make himself better off by stealing the cattle of others. And every indication is that the Nuer are tempted to do so. They certainly raid the livestock of neighboring tribes; thus, the last sentence of our first quotation from Evans-Pritchard reads in full: "Cattle are their dearest possession and [the Nuer] gladly risk their lives to . . . pillage those of their neighbors."[6] The strength of their desire to steal is further suggested by Evans-Pritchard when he recounts: "As my Nuer servant once said to me: 'You can trust a Nuer with any amount of money, pounds and pounds and pounds, and go away for years and return and he will not have stolen it; but a single cow – that is a different matter'."[7]

---

[4] Ibid., p. 16. [5] Ibid. [6] Ibid., p. 16, italics mine.

[7] Ibid., p. 49. Several readers have, in effect, argued at this point, "You don't convince me. Maybe the Nuer are not like us. Maybe they find it unthinkable to steal cattle from other Nuer. Maybe they would experience great shame if they did so, and so not enjoy the cattle they stole. For such reasons, maybe there isn't much of a problem of order among the Nuer, and thus no reason to pursue the topic of this paper."

I have several counter-arguments. First, Evans-Pritchard delimits the boundary of the society in terms of the area within which disputes can be peacefully resolved; the group is thus distinguished by the existence of mechanisms for the peaceful resolution of conflict rather than by the absence of conflict, as the commentators would have it. Second, any reading of the material on the Nuer reveals them to be as contentious and greedy as the rest of us; it was in part because this was the case that Evans-Pritchard was motivated to study how they managed to avoid social conflict. Third, in so far as the readers argue that the existence of a moral community weakens the incentives to harm others, as opposed to

The puzzle, from Evans-Pritchard's point of view, was that, despite the potential for theft and disorder, the Nuer in fact tended to live in relative harmony. In so far as the Nuer raided cattle, they tended to raid the cattle of others; raids within the tribe were relatively rare.[8] Somehow the Nuer appear to have avoided the potentially harmful effects arising from the pursuit of self-interest in the absence of those institutions so common to states: the courts, the police, and the judiciary.

In discussing Evans-Pritchard's analysis, we can credibly abstract his account in a number of forms. Gluckman's celebrated treatment, which we will discuss, highlights the role of interested parties and cross-cutting cleavages – a notion of conflict regulation that is familiar to political scientists of the sociological persuasion.[9] In this chapter, we highlight the structure of conflict in a way that is more relevant to those interested in political economy and portray it in the form of a two-person, non-cooperative, variable-sum game, traditionally known as the prisoners' dilemma.[10]

While doing so, we conceive of the situation of two property-holding units, each of families I and II, and assume that both own ten cattle. Each family can choose between two alternatives: using force to gain more cattle or remaining passive and non-violent. Each knows that the other family faces a similar choice. And each knows what the results of each choice will be.

eradicating them entirely, I would agree with their point and therefore address it in the last portion of the chapter.

[8] P. P. Howell, 1954, *A Manual of Nuer Law*. London: Oxford University Press for the International African Institute, pp. 200–201.

[9] See ch. 1 of Max Gluckman, 1960, *Custom and Conflict in Africa*. Oxford: Basil Blackwell.

[10] For other efforts to apply game theory to anthropology, see Frederik Barth, 1959, "Segmentary Opposition and the Theory of Games: A Study of Pathan Organization." *Journal of the Royal Anthropological Society* 89, 5–22; and Martin Southwold, 1969, "A Games Model of African Tribal Politics," in Ira R. Buchler and Hugo G. Nutini, eds., *Game Theory in the Behavioral Sciences*. Pittsburgh: University of Pittsburgh Press. For reviews, see the contribution in Buchler and Nutini, eds., *Game Theory*, and also the articles by Anthony P. Glascock, 1975, "Optimization Theory and the Analysis of Political Behavior." *Political Anthropology* 1, 136–154; and Douglas R. White, 1979, "Mathematical Anthropology," in John J. Honigman, ed., *Handbook of Social and Cultural Anthropology*. Chicago: Rand-McNally. For formulations that have strongly influenced the development of this essay, see also Frederick G. Bailey, 1969, *Stratagems and Spoils: A Social Anthropology of Politics*. New York: Schocken; and Charles R. Plott and Robert A. Meyer, 1975, "The Technology of Public Goods, Externalities, and the Exclusion Principle," in Edwin S. Mills, ed., *Economic Analysis of Environmental Problems*. New York: National Bureau of Economic Research.

Both families know that should they abjure the use of force, each will continue to enjoy the possession of ten cattle. But both also know that raiding is profitable. Should family I raid family II's herd whilst family II failed to resist, it could appropriate eight of family II's cattle, we shall assume; similarly, should family II raid family I and family I not forcibly resist, family II could gain eight cattle at family I's expense. Both also know that in the face of a raid from each other, there are gains to those who resist, even though they may pay a price in physical suffering. For purposes of argument, assume that wounds, the breakdown of herding during the course of battle, and property damage result in losses equivalent to six cattle. In any case, this outcome is to be preferred to not using force to protect one's herds, for then eight cattle are lost to the predatory party.

The situation is summarized in Figure 2.1. The choices for family I are listed on the left: F designates the choice of force and $\bar{F}$ designates the renunciation of force. The choices for family II are similar and are listed at the top of the table. The entries refer to the outcomes for the paired choices of families I and II, the value of the outcomes being expressed in terms of numbers of cattle, and the value to family I being listed first and the value to family II being listed second.[11]

The nature of the dilemma is clear. It is rational for each family to choose to use force; indeed, each does best employing force *no matter what* the choice of the other. Moreover, it is also clear that the use of force is a stable outcome. When both families use force, then the situation is in equilibrium, for it is in neither family's interest to renounce it. Were family I unilaterally to abjure the use of force, for example, then its holdings would drop from four cattle to two and the same is true of family II.

		Π	
		F	$\bar{F}$
I	F	4,4	18,2
	$\bar{F}$	2,18	10,10

FIGURE 2.1 Payoffs to families I and II for choice of strategies

---

[11] It should be noted that, by all accounts, the Nuer do translate physical pain and suffering and even death into cattle equivalents. See Evans-Pritchard, *The Nuer*, p. 127, and Howell, *A Manual of Nuer Law*, pp. 25–48.

Moreover, no other choice is in equilibrium. The equilibrium outcome is thus unique.

What is peculiar and compelling, however, is the nature of this outcome. Under it, *both families are worse off*. Had they renounced the use of force, they would each have had ten cattle but they now get only four. It would seem that among the Nuer, everyone would be better off living peacefully, but no one can afford to live that way. The structure of the prisoners' dilemma thus captures the fragility of social order, and does so in a particularly compelling manner.

Thus the problem that Evans-Pritchard confronted: In the absence of a state, how can the Nuer live in peace? Addressing this question, he pursued two lines of reasoning. One was to look at the role of mechanisms for conflict resolution and dispute settlement. The second was to explore other facets of Nuer culture – ones that altered, in effect, the incentives that threatened the cohesion of Nuer society.

CONFLICT RESOLUTION

Compensation

While explaining how the Nuer attained political order, Evan-Pritchard placed strong emphasis upon the role of compensation. In this section, we examine how such a convention might work.

Assume that a system of compensation is available and observe the incentives that then face someone who might be contemplating the use of force. Say that family I is pondering whether to raid the herds of family II. Family I knows that family II gets to choose not only between the use of force and non-violence but also between those two alternatives and a third: having its cattle returned while exacting two cattle as compensation. Let $\overline{F}C$ stand for this option of no-force-with-compensation. The decisional problem now reads as in Figure 2.2.

Family I now must confront the possibility that, if it attacks, family II will exact compensation; in that case, family I will be less well off than if it did not attack (it will have eight cattle instead of ten), and the incentives to attack are weakened. Moreover, family II is better off exacting compensation than it is resisting by force (it gets twelve cattle instead of four); and, if it knows that family I will also seek compensation if attacked, it has little incentive itself to raid the herds of family I. The possibility of compensation thus reduces the incentives

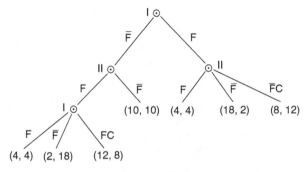

FIGURE 2.2 Adding payoffs for compensation

for violence. Both families will find it in their interests to live peacefully and enjoy their ten cattle.[12]

Procedures for compensation thus alter the incentives faced by the two parties and do so in such a way that it is no longer in their interests to choose the use of violence. And thus it is that Evans-Pritchard perceptively delineates that area within which compensation is paid from that area within which vengeance is taken. The former he regards as a political community that he terms "a tribe." Within it exist institutions that reduce the incentives for violence, thus making order possible.[13]

Arbitration

Equally central to Evans-Pritchard's analysis of the attainment of social order is his stress on the role of arbitration; I refer, of course, to his discussion of the leopard-skin chief. In the political analyses inspired by Evans-Pritchard's work, few subjects have provoked as much attention as his discussion of this figure. And among the principal controversies have been debates concerning his source of influence.

Some, such as Greuel, have argued that the influence of the chief arises from his capacity to coerce;[14] Haight partially subscribes to this position, arguing that in those areas "where members of the leopard-skin chief lineage were also members of the dominant lineage," and in those situations when a leopard-skin chief was also a "senior kinsman," the chief

---

[12] A keen-eyed reader will no doubt discern a moral hazard in this system of compensation. See the discussion in note 21.

[13] Evans-Pritchard, *The Nuer*, pp. 121ff.

[14] Peter J. Greuel, 1971, "The Leopard-Skin Chief: An Examination of Political Power Among the Nuer." *American Anthropologist* 73, 1115–1120.

thus had the power to compel the settlement of disputes.[15] But Greuel, Haight, and others who stress the power to coerce are simply missing the compelling quality of the Nuer case: the striking absence of the Weberian attribute of "stateness." The evidence for this is far too strong to be ignored, and Evans-Pritchard could not have made the point more clearly:

I have never seen Nuer treat a chief with more respect than they treat other people or speak of them as persons of much importance. They regard them as agents through whom disputes of a certain kind can be effaced ... and I have often heard remarks such as this: 'We took hold of them and gave them leopard skins and made them our chiefs.'[16]

Likewise [the chief] has no means of compelling the people to pay or to accept blood-cattle. He has no powerful kinsmen or the backing of a populous community to support him. He is simply a mediator in a specific social situation.[17]

Others have explored the normative, as opposed to the physical, element of the influence of the leopard-skin chief. Opposing the elements of legitimacy and power in their explorations of chiefly authority, scholars such as Burton and Beidelman emphasize the significance of the moral basis of political suasion. They stress in particular the capacity of the leopard-skin chief to evoke the primacy of moral considerations in private choice, thereby eliciting a social consciousness on the part of private individuals.[18]

The discussion of the role of morality in social conflict is of obvious importance and will receive attention in later stages of this analysis. But just as invoking the capacity for coercion misses out on Evans-Pritchard's analysis of arbitration, so invoking the capacity for virtuous behavior trivializes his investigation into how socially coherent behavior can be evoked from self-interested individuals.

In the case of the Nuer, he shows, social coherence comes neither from the organic immersion of individual preferences into an ethical order nor

[15] Bruce Haight, 1972, "A Note on the Leopard-Skin Chief." *American Anthropologist* 74, 1316.

[16] Evans-Prichard, *The Nuer*, p. 173.

[17] Ibid., p. 174. For further discussions, see E. E. Evans-Pritchard, 1956, *Nuer Religion*. Oxford: The Clarendon Press, pp. 109–110, 290ff, and 300. See also Howell, *A Manual of Nuer Law*, pp. 43–44.

[18] John W. Burton, 1974, "Some Nuer Notions of Purity and Danger: Dedicated to the Memory of E. E. Evans-Pritchard (1902–1973)," *Anthropos* 69, (3–4), 517–536; John W. Burton, 1978, "Living with the Dead: Aspects of the Afterlife in Nuer and Dinka Cosmology (Sudan)." *Anthropos* 73, 1–2, 141–160; T. O. Beidelman, 1971, "Nuer Priests and Prophets: Charisma, Authority and Power among the Nuer," in T. O. Beidelman, ed., *The Translation of Culture*. London: Tavistock, pp. 375–415.

from the Hobbesian alternative of coerced compliance; rather, it emerges as a by-product, so to speak, of self-interested choice-making by rational individuals.

The role of the leopard-skin chief, Evans-Pritchard emphasizes, is to serve as a communication link between conflicting parties. The offended party, it would appear, communicates two basic messages: (1) either we receive compensation or we exact vengeance, and (2) an idea of an adequate level of compensation. The offending party responds by communicating his assessment of adequate compensation. And subsequent interchanges appear largely to represent bargaining sessions in which the level of compensation is negotiated.

Figure 2.2 illustrates the process. Say family I has used violence and family II has yet to undertake reprisals. The two families are at a point in which the distribution of payoffs is 18, 2. Through the leopard-skin chief, family II offers family I a choice of two alternatives: revenge with payoffs 4, 4, or restitution and some form of compensation, ideally (from its point of view) with payoffs of 8, 12. The threat of forceful revenge will be a credible one as family II can gain thereby. So long as the message – pay up or suffer the consequences – is transmitted in a credible fashion (and care is taken to ensure that it is)[19] violence is not really at issue. What is at issue is the final level of compensation: that is, how far family II can improve its position and to what extent family I can hold on to its ill-gotten gains. By communicating family II's unambivalent intention to inflict harm, and by serving as a go-between in the bargaining over compensation, the leopard-skin chief appears to facilitate this bargaining and contributes to the peaceful resolution of the dispute.[20]

---

[19] See the display of threatening behavior that takes place during the period of arbitration as recorded in Evans-Pritchard, *The Nuer*, p. 153.

[20] Several other properties of this process warrant comment. First, as much as possible, the Nuer render the leopard-skin chief an "impartial" arbiter. Thus, he is a relatively poor person with no large cattle holdings; he is therefore less likely to be a party to disputes or to have a stake in their outcomes. This argument has been contested by Greuel ("The Leopard-Skin Chief") who contended that the leopard-skin chief amassed large cattle holdings. I must agree with Haight ("A Note on the Leopard-Skin Chief"), however, that Greuel's contention finds little support in Evans-Pritchard's data. Second, it is clear that the limits of the bargain should insure that neither party does better after violence than before. In particular, family II should not be allowed to gain more than ten cattle; for then it will have an incentive to entice family I to aggress and then to assess damages.

In the jargon of political economy, the creation of such an incentive would represent a "moral hazard." Moral hazards arise when arrangements that are designed to correct social problems in fact create incentives which exacerbate them; insuring against the risks of automobile accidents, for example, may lead to less careful driving and thus to a higher

SOCIAL AND CULTURAL FOUNDATIONS FOR PEACE

Compensation and arbitration are thus central mechanisms for the preservation of order among the Nuer, according to Evans-Pritchard. And yet we must wonder how these mechanisms are maintained. Especially in the absence of formal institutions capable of apprehending evaders of the law, we would expect persons to refuse to abide by these mechanisms of dispute settlement. But they do not appear to do so. As Evans-Pritchard makes clear, the Nuer in fact willingly employ these mechanisms and, by and large, tend to submit to whatever outcomes the mechanisms may dictate; and it is only the fact that the Nuer willingly do so, he argues, that makes these mechanisms work.[21] Considerations such as these lead us to seek more fundamental factors that may be at work – factors that would transform the payoff matrix being viewed by the Nuer in such a way that the incentives to use force are substantially altered and the compelling power of the prisoners' dilemma is weakened.

DETERRENCE

Evans-Pritchard repeatedly emphasizes the role of threats of violence in securing social peace. The very readiness of the Nuer to use violence, he argues, is a reason why it is not employed. By his account, the Nuer appreciate the role of deterrence and know that they must unambiguously and forcefully communicate their willingness to fight in order to prevent predation and the general social turmoil that then results. As he states: "It is the knowledge that a Nuer is brave and will stand up against aggression and enforce his rights by club and spear that ensures respect for person and property."[22] This point achieves further importance in Evans-Pritchard's delimitation of zones of peace and violence in Nuer society. It is precisely in those zones in which a man can recruit kin support to engage in battle and thus credibly threaten reprisal, he contends, that disputes are most likely to be settled peacefully.[23]

---

frequency of accidents. It is interesting to note that the Nuer appear to be aware of this class of problems. For example, the ethnographic accounts suggest that they take great pains to insure that the families of women do not benefit substantially from cattle paid in damages for adultery or premarital impregnations; they do so by placing restrictions on the use that can be made of such cattle (see Evans-Pritchard, *Nuer Religion*, pp. 186–187). See also the discussion in Howell, *A Manual of Nuer Law*, p. vii.

[21] Evans-Pritchard, *The Nuer*, pp. 174ff.

[22] Ibid., pp. 170–171. See also Howell, *A Manual of Nuer Law*, pp. 23ff, 39.

[23] Evans-Pritchard, *The Nuer*, pp. 150ff; also Howell, *A Manual of Nuer Law*, pp. 24, 41.

Π

		F	F̄
I	F	4,4	0,0
	F̄	0,0	10,10

FIGURE 2.3 Payoffs with retaliation

Π

		F	R	F̄
I	F	4,4	4,4	18,2
	R	4,4	10,10	10,10
	F̄	2,18	10,10	10,10

FIGURE 2.4 Payoffs with contingent use of force

In recasting Evans-Pritchard's account into a choice-making framework we can interpret it in two ways. One is to view his argument as contending that threats represent an informational strategy aimed at modifying an opponent's perception of one's probable behavior. In essence, threats transform the payoff matrix; they remove the off-diagonal cells by communicating that these payoffs will occur with probability zero. The new payoff matrix appears as in Figure 2.3.

Given this perception of the payoffs to alternative behaviors, both parties, behaving rationally, will choose the option of non-violence.

Evans-Pritchard's account can be interpreted in another fashion. Once again, the payoff matrix is altered and again in a way that removes the structure of incentives that generates socially harmful choice-making by rational individuals. The existence of threats can be held to generate an expansion of the set of strategies to include not only the use or abnegation of force but also the contingent use of force (i.e. the use of force only as a form of reprisal). When the parties to potential disputes can elect this option – here labeled alternative R (for retaliation) – then the payoff matrix would appear as in Figure 2.4.

By contrast with Figure 2.1, the use of force here does *not* represent a dominant strategy; it does not represent a choice which is unconditionally best (i.e. best no matter what the choice of the other family). Moreover, the choice of the strategy of reprisal, R, by both parties is stable; were each family to choose to use force only if force were employed by the other family, then neither would have an incentive unilaterally to alter its behavior. In the face of such credible threats, it is thus possible for both parties, behaving rationally, to choose not to use force, and for this state of affairs – peace within the feud – to persist.

Crosscutting Ties

It was Gluckman who coined the phrase "peace in the feud." In a noted review essay thus entitled, Gluckman reappraised Evans-Pritchard's classic in the light of subsequent anthropological research.[24] He based his analysis primarily upon Elizabeth Colson's studies of the Plateau Tonga, in which she stressed the multiple interests that bind together members of small-scale societies.[25] These ties, he argued after Colson, appear to provide means of inflicting penalties that weaken the incentives to cause harm to others; they also appear to weaken the incentives for forceful retribution and to strengthen the incentives for compensation. In effect, they represent social institutions that alter the incentives that structure the choices made by conflicting members of society.

Rules of exogamy and dispersed residence represent two such social institutions. In Colson's essay, for example, she emphasizes the role women played in mediating a dispute between two clans. A murder had been committed and the parties to the dispute were on the verge of violent conflict. Because of exogamous rules of marriage, however, the daughters and sisters of the members of one clan were to be found as the wives of members of the other. The lobbying effort of the women promoted a peaceful resolution of the conflict; the pressures they exerted forestalled the threat of violence.[26]

Gluckman conjectures that dispersed residence promotes similar behavior among the Nuer. Members of a given family do not cluster in a single village; they tend to be widely dispersed. When an injury is inflicted by one family upon another, the dispute is therefore likely to divide the residents of villages. But in so far as the residents of a village cannot cooperate, their interests suffer. Acting as residents of common

---

[24] The essay appears in Max Gluckman, 1960, *Custom and Conflict in Africa.* Oxford: Basil Blackwell.

[25] See Elizabeth Colson, 1970, "Social Control and Vengeance in Plateau Tonga Society" in her *The Plateau Tonga of Northern Rhodesia (Zambia): Social and Religious Studies.* Manchester: The Institute for Social Research, University of Zambia.

[26] Ibid., pp. 102–121.

villages, members of opposing families may therefore champion a quick and peaceful settlement of the conflict that divides them.[27]

Gluckman's argument concerning crosscutting ties – be they ties of marriage or of common residence – thus implies that social institutions can impose costs upon those who would choose to utilize violence. In discussing the effect of exogamous marriage, for example, Gluckman notes:

> When a man has got a wife from another group, he has an interest in being friends with that group ... It's not just sentiment. A woman remains attached to her own kin, and if her husband quarrels with them she can make life pretty unpleasant for him ... A man's brother-in-law is maternal uncle to his children, and by custom is required to assist them in many critical situations. He can bless his nephew, and his curse is believed to be among the worst, if not the worst, a Nuer can receive, for, unlike the father, a maternal uncle may curse a youth's cattle, as well as his crops and fishing and hunting, if he is disobedient or refuses a request or in some other way offends him. The curse may also prevent the nephew from begetting male children. So for the welfare of his family, and the prosperity of his children, each man is led by his interests ... to seek to be on good terms with his wife's kin.[28]

Similarly, given family dispersion, the decision to use violence leads to the loss of aid in herding, billeting, food acquisition and preparation, and access to water – resources that are distributed by neighborhood groups which, given the nature of Nuer institutions, recruit their members from a variety of families.

Social institutions too alter the nature of the payoff matrix in Figure 2.1. Should the interests at stake be particularly strong, the payoffs will be transformed so that they no longer pose a prisoners' dilemma. Say, for example, that the losses experienced by the force-employing party in terms of those 'other interests' (be they conjugal or residential in nature) are worth the equivalent of nine cattle; then, as shown in Figure 2.5, the renunciation of force is a dominant strategy, an equilibrium exists $(\overline{F}, \overline{F})$, and it is a social optimum.

---

[27] See Gluckman, *Custom and Conflict*, pp. 11–12. Gluckman's conjecture is supported by the evidence of ritual avoidance between Nuer families involved in a dispute, particularly a homicide. Evans-Pritchard comments, for example: "Until the blood-feud is closed ... the kin of the slayer and the slain may not eat or drink from vessels from which the other has eaten or drunk ... Even to use the same vessels at the home of a third party who is in no way connected with the feud may entail the most serious consequences. A third party may cause death to one side or the other by eating or drinking with both" (*Nuer Religion*, p. 179; see also p. 294 and Howell, *A Manual of Nuer Law*, p. 220). Given the necessity for such a high degree of avoidance, the disruptions of neighborhood life occasioned by disputes must have been extremely high, and so too the incentives for their resolution.

[28] Gluckman, *Custom and Conflict*, p. 13.

Societies without States

Π

		F	F̄
I	F	−5,−5	9,2
	F̄	2,9	10,10

FIGURE 2.5 When players have other interests

Π

		F	F̄
I	F	3,3	17,2
	F̄	2,17	10,10

FIGURE 2.6 When other interests are of little value

Π

		F	F̄	F̄R
I	F	4,4	17,2	9,10
	F̄	2,17	10,10	10,10
	F̄R	10,9	10,10	10,10

FIGURE 2.7 Payoffs when there is restitution

If the "other interests" are not particularly strong, the parties to the dispute may well remain locked in a prisoners' dilemma situation; this is illustrated in Figure 2.6, where those who use force experience a loss in other interests equivalent to the value of one cow.

Nonetheless, because of the weakened incentive to use force, lower levels of compensation are required to alter the incentives to aggress, and the control of disputes is thus more easily obtained. Thus, as shown in Figure 2.7, applying a rule of restitution – merely that the appropriate cattle must be returned in full – makes the renunciation of force (with restitution) a preferred strategy for parties who have been aggressed upon.

Figure 2.7 helps to point out that when force is costly in terms of its effect on other interests, it is easier to devise a mechanism of compensation that will incorporate incentives for the preservation of peace. And this appears to be the core of the crosscutting ties argument.

Religious Beliefs

There is a last factor that has been used to explain the existence of social cohesion among the Nuer, and this is their religion.

Nuer religion has been studied by Evans-Pritchard himself, by Beidelman and by Burton.[29] Insight into the religious values of the Nuer comes from studying their theories of misfortune; and these, it would appear, share common traits with the beliefs of other societies. Personal misfortune, it is held, can result from ill-feeling, which in turn can be caused by being harmed. Thus, if one person has injured another, but not in a way that generates formal compensation and restitution, the offender is still liable to be punished; for as Gluckman states, "bad feeling is charged with mystical danger."[30]

One way of inflicting misfortune among the Nuer is through the curse. Evans-Pritchard discussed the role of the curse in the following terms:

The curse is undoubtedly a powerful sanction of conduct, largely because it is not thought necessary that a wronged man should utter it aloud for misfortune to follow. He has only to think it. Such an unspoken curse Nuer call a *biit loac*, a curse of the heart. Indeed, it would seem that he need not expressly formulate a curse in his mind at all, a mere feeling of resentment arising from a genuine grievance being sufficient to cause injury to the person who occasioned it.[31]

The incentives for forceful appropriation are thus reduced, for the material gains are made at the cost of generating anger, which in turn can lead to one's death, illness, or misfortune. As Gluckman states: "The beliefs exert ... pressure on men and women to observe the social virtues. ... The beliefs support the moral order of the community."[32]

A variant of this belief is the conviction that private acts can have public consequences. The occurrence of collective misfortunes, for example, provokes inquiries into unresolved private grievances and undisclosed misdemeanors. Drought, plague, or a series of lesser disasters may suggest the existence of an uncompensated injury, and the beliefs covering collective misfortune thus help to vest personal property rights more securely. For example, Evans-Pritchard reports: "To kill a man and not to confess to the killing is a heinous offense in Nuer eyes because it puts the kin on

---

[29] Evans-Pritchard, *Nuer Religion*; Beidelman, "Nuer Priests and Prophets"; and Burton, "Some Nuer Notions of Purity and Danger."

[30] Gluckman, *Custom and Conflict*, p. 94.   [31] Evans-Pritchard, *Nuer Religion*, p. 170.

[32] Gluckman, *Custom and Conflict*, p. 94.

both sides in jeopardy."[33] An unpropitiated ghost, in Nuer beliefs, is extremely dangerous.[34] As Burton states,

Those recently deceased are ... thought to hold the same feelings toward the living as was the case when they were alive. ... While normally a number of months elapse between burial and the mortuary ceremony, it is understandable why the Nuer should think of the power of the deceased to seek vengeance ... to be especially strong in the interim.[35]

The obvious correlative of such beliefs is that care should be taken to insure that persons are not injured (lest they die with a grievance in their hearts) and that transgressions and injuries should be reported and dealt with (presumably prior to the victim's demise). Failing such measures, the collectivity is liable to calamitous misfortune.

While Burton and others stress the difference between the religious beliefs of different African societies and the variations in their impact upon social behavior, sufficient commonalities none the less remain to suggest a common core. Goldschmidt's study of the Sebei represents a case in point. Goldschimdt reports that a clan, upon the death of *one* of its members, held an inquiry into the behavior of *all* of its members. It sought to determine recent transgressions that could have engendered sufficient resentment to provoke a death. Cases of possible theft, arson, adultery, and such were examined. "They listed no fewer than seven possible sources of the evil influences that were invading them," Goldschmidt contends; "a wide range in circumstances ... could ... operate as a source of death."[36] Inquiries were made, he reports, and the grievances were settled; the social and moral order was thereby restored.

Thus, the beliefs of the Nuer, and of other societies, may be such as to alter the perceived gains to be made from forceful appropriation. They provide incentives to curtail those who may seek to take advantage of the absence of formal institutions.

CONCLUSION

In many agrarian societies, control over the means of violence rests in private hands. Instead of security being provided by formal institutions, it

---

[33] Evans-Pritchard, *Nuer Religion*, p. 297.   [34] Ibid., pp. 173–175.
[35] Burton, "Living with the Dead," p. 145.
[36] Walter Goldschmidt, 1967, *Sebei Law*. Berkeley and Los Angeles: University of California Press, pp. 83–87.

is instead provided by private families. It is the fear of reprisal that keeps the peace.

Hark back to the payoffs in the matrices above. Now let development proceed. As prosperity increases, so too, you will find, does the temptation to steal. In societies governed by kin, we learn, increasing prosperity fuels increasing insecurity. In the chapter that follows we dig deeper and learn one of the most important lessons of this work: that when control over the means of violence remains in private hands, there can be no development. To remain prosperous, one must be prepared to fight; to be secure, it is best to have nothing worth stealing. Thereafter, we switch our attention to societies in which the means of violence are controlled by a central political hierarchy. We switch our attention to the state.

3

An Impossibility Result?

The study of development draws upon two sets of data. One is drawn from the contemporary cross section of human societies; thus we turned to Evans-Pritchard's study of the Nuer who inhabit what is now South Sudan. The second is drawn from history: we compare societies that today are prosperous and industrial with what they were like when still poor and agrarian. Data from both sources suggest that societies without states cannot remain orderly while becoming prosperous. They are unable, that is, to develop.

To understand why, in this chapter, we focus on private individuals as they allocate their resources between production, leisure, and fighting and lay the foundations for this argument.

KINSHIP POLITIES

In many agrarian societies, people are neither farmers nor warriors but rather possess the capabilities of each. They allocate their resources between production, military activities, and "leisure." That they do so suggests the structure of a model – one that we can use to explore the relationship between political order and economic prosperity.

This chapter is based upon Robert Bates, Avner Greif, and Smita Singh, 2002, "Organizing Violence." *Journal of Conflict Resolution* 46(5) (October), 599–628. Transforming the original article into a chapter for a book led to the re-writing of portions of the text. These alterations do not affect the arguments originally advanced.

The Model

For simplicity, we focus on the behavior of two players who can be individuals, families, or groups of kin.[1] Each player is labeled i, where i = 1, 2. And each possesses resources, denoted by T_i, that he or she can allocate between work (w_i), military preparedness (m_i), and leisure (l_i). In each period

$$i \epsilon \{1,2\} \ chooses \ w_i, m_i, l_i \geq 0 \ \text{s.t.} \ w_i + m_i + l_i = T. \tag{1}$$

The resources devoted to working, w_i, result in an output of $F(w_i)$ for player I, which can be construed as wealth or income.[2]

After allocating their resources, each player observes the decision of the other and then (sequentially) decides whether to turn to violence. To capture this decision, define $r_i = \{0, 1\}$ to equal 1 if player i raids and 0 if she does not and let player 1 choose first.

Raiding is costly and requires k units of output. The amount one can gain from raiding depends on one's relative strength. If player i attacks and player –i defends, then $M(m_i, m_{-i})$ is the share of player –i's wealth that player i is able to expropriate if she allocates m_i units and player –i m_{-i} to their respective military. If a player does not invest in her military capabilities, she cannot gain from raiding and the more the one invests relative to the other, the greater her return from raiding. By the same token, the more a player devotes her resources to defense, the more difficult it is for others to expropriate her wealth.[3] $M(m_i, m_{-i})$ thus

---

[1] Having more players would make the first best less likely and the noncooperative equilibrium more likely, thus strengthening our argument. Note that we ignore issues arising from the internal politics of families.

[2] $F(\cdot)$ is assumed to be a twice continuously differentiable, concave function that maps from player i's effort to her or his income.

[3] The following is assumed with respect to the function M : (a)$M\epsilon[0,1]$. Obviously, no player can expropriate more than what the other possesses. (b) $= \partial M/\partial m_i \geq 0 \ and \ \partial M/\partial m_{-i} \leq 0; \partial^2 m/\partial m_i 2 \leq 0 \ and \ \partial^2 M/\partial m_{-i} 2 \geq 0$. M is nondecreasing in m_i and nonincreasing in m_{-i}. It is a twice continuously differentiable function with decreasing returns, which means that the portion of player –i's wealth that player i can expropriate is concave in m_i and convex in m_{-i}. (c) $M > 0$ if $m_i > 0$. That is, if and only if player i invests in military ability can she or he expropriate part of the other player's income. (d)$\partial^2 M/\partial m_i \partial m_{-i} < 0$. The cross-partial derivative of M with respect to m_i and m_{-1} is negative. That is, the more military ability a person acquires, the more she or he is able to engage in defense and the more difficult it is to expropriate her or his wealth. For a general analysis of such contest functions, see Stergios Skaperdas, 1996a, "Contest Success Functions." *Economic Theory* 7, 283–290.

captures the balance of military capabilities and the resultant level of redistribution.[4]

Payoffs to the players are a product of their allocation of time and effort to working, leisure, and the enhancement of their military prowess. They are given for each i by

$$I_1 = F(w_1) + r_1\Big(F(w_2)M(m_1, m_2) - k\Big) - r_2[F(w_1) \\ + r_1\Big(F(w_2)M(m_1, m_2) - k\Big)]M(m_2, m_1).$$

and

$$I_2 = F(w_2) - r_1\Big(F(w_2)M(m_1, m_2)\Big) + r_2\Big([F(w_1) + r_1\Big(F(w_2)\Big) \\ M(m_1, m_2) - k)]M(m_2, m_1) - k\Big).$$

---

[4] We ignore the possibility that one agent can eliminate the other. We do so because we want to consider stateless societies in which there are ongoing, possibly violent, interactions between groups – be they tribes, communities, lineages, or villages. Similarly, we do not consider a situation in which one gains military resources by raiding the other. When this is the case, one group is likely to come to dominate the other.

One can therefore consider our analysis as addressing a situation in which property rights are determined endogenously through interactions between two players. The degree to which one can secure property rights depends on relative coercive capabilities.

The model ignores, for simplicity's sake, potentially important aspects of conflict situations of the sort we seek to explore. It puts to the side, for example, evolutionary forces and specialization in the use of violence (as in Boaz Moselle and Ben Polak, 1999, "Anarchy, Organized Crime, and Extortion: A Cynical Theory of the State." Paper presented at the Conference on Political Violence, Princeton University, Princeton, NJ); asymmetries among the agents (as in, e.g., Herschel I. Grossman and Minseong Kim, 1995, "Swords or Ploughshares? A Theory of the Security Claims to Property." *Journal of Political Economy* 103, 1275–1288; and Abhinay Muthoo, 2000, "On the Foundations of Property Rights, Part I: A Model of the State-of-Nature with Two Players." Department of Economics, Essex. Typescript); the impact of past conflicts on one's current military capabilities (discussed in James D. Fearon, 1996, "Bargaining over Objects That Influence Future Bargaining Power." Paper presented at the 1997 annual meeting of the American Political Science Association, Washington, DC); uncertainty and loss of potential exchange (discussed in Stergios Skaperdas, 1996b, "Gangs and the State of Nature," in P. Newman, ed., *The New Palgrave Dictionary of Economics and the Law.* London: Palgrave); and moral hazard issues (explored in Tony Addison, Philippe Le Billon, and S. Mansoob Murshed, 2000, "Conflict in Africa: The Cost of Peaceful Behavior." Working paper, WIDER, Helsinki, Finland).

By the same token, this framework enables us to extend the analysis beyond that achieved in these works. Specifically, it allows us to examine the endogenous determination of prosperity and violence. The model in Muthoo (2000) is closest to ours. Although it explores the impact of asymmetries (which we do not), it does not enable agents to invest in military capabilities, as do we. Nor does it allow us to explore such issues as deterring raids, as by consuming leisure.

Analysis

Employing this framework, we first explore equilibria that can form in a single period and then those that can form in an infinitely repeated version of the game. Doing so we find:

1. That in societies in which coercion is privately deployed for raiding and protection, behavior in equilibrium is likely to entail the unproductive use of resources in military preparations and activity. The first best allocation of resources between work and leisure is therefore unlikely to prevail. We call this equilibrium an anarchy equilibrium. This is the equilibrium achieved in kinship polities, such as the Nuer.
2. That the greater the prosperity of a stateless society, and the more productive the technology of production $F(\bullet)$, the less likely is the first best allocation to prevail without investment in the means of violence.
3. That an equilibrium with positive investments in military capabilities can Pareto dominate the optimal equilibrium with none.
4. And that to escape from the trade-off between peace and prosperity that thus characterize kinship societies, such societies might seek the introduction of a centralized form of political order – something that would enable them to develop.

We now derive these implications from the model.

A SINGLE-SHOT FRAMEWORK

The first best allocation of resources, (w^*, l^*), represents a solution to the problem:

$$\max_{w, l \geq 0, w + l = T} U\Big(F(w), l\Big).$$

We wish to compare this allocation with that achieved in equilibrium. Before doing so, we first need to explore the conditions that yield subgame perfection in this game.[5]

---

[5] In which $w_i = w^*$, $m_i = 0$, $l_i = l^*$.

Preliminaries

Define r_2 as taking the value 1 when $\{[F(w_1) + r_1(F(w_2)M(m_1, m_2) - k)]$ $M(m_2, m_1) > k\}$ and the value 0 otherwise.

Denote the resulting indicator function as $R_2(w_1, w_2, m_1, m_2, r_1)$. Using this expression, we can express I_1 as a function of only w_1, w_2, m_1, m_2, and r_1.[6]

Choices

Given w_2, m_2, l_2, player 1 solves optimization problem (1):

$$\max_{w, m, l \geq 0, \ w+m+l=T} U\left(\begin{array}{l} F(w) + R_1(w, w_2, m, m_2)\Big(F(w_2)M(m, m_2) - k\Big) \\ -R_2\Big(w, w_2, m, m_2, R_1()[F(w) + R_1(w, w_2, m, m_2) \\ \Big(F(w_2)M(m, m_2) - k\Big)]M(m_2, m)\Big), l \end{array}\right). \tag{1}$$

Likewise, given w_1, m_1, l_1, player 2 solves optimization problem (2)

$$\max_{w, m, l \geq 0, \ w+m+l=T} U\left(\begin{array}{l} F(w) + R_1(w_1, w, m_1, m)\Big(F(w)M(m_1, m)\Big) \\ +R_2\Big(w_1, w, m_1, m, R_1()([F(w_1) + R_1(w_1, w, m_1, m) \\ \Big(F(w)M(m_1, m) - k\Big)]M(m, m_1) - k\Big), l \end{array}\right). \tag{2}$$

A solution to these two equations constitutes a subgame perfect equilibrium (SPE) in this game.

Implications

We now can address the question: under what conditions would that equilibrium support the first best allocation? That is, under what conditions would $w_i = w^*$, $m_i = 0$, $l_i = l^* \ \forall \ I$ prevail?

Addressing this question, we find that if $m_i = 0$, then $r_i = 0$ is a strictly dominant strategy. If one did not invest any resources in military ability in the first substage, then raiding would yield no gains. Indeed, the predator would lose at least k, the fixed cost of raiding. In considering the conditions for a subgame perfect equilibrium, we therefore need only to consider deviations that begin in the first stage of the game.

---

[6] Hence, $r_1 = 1 \{I_1(w_1, w_2, m_1, m_2, 1) > I_1(w_1, w_2, m_1, m_2, 0)\}$, which we denote by $R1(w_1, w_2, m_1, m_2)$.

Because military activity diverts resources from production and leisure, a deviation would be profitable only if it also involves raiding. A necessary and sufficient condition for the first best to prevail as a subgame perfect equilibrium is therefore that for $\forall i$

$$\max_{w,\,m,\,l \geq 0,\, w+m+l=T} U\Big(F(w) + \big(F(w^*)M(m,0) - k,l\big)\Big) \leq U\big(F(w^*),l^*\big).$$

For this condition to hold, it must be the case that

$$\max_{w,\,m,\,l \geq 0,\, w+m+l=T} \{(F(w) + (F(w^*)M(m,0) - k\} \leq F(w^*).$$

Even if one player has devoted nothing to increase her military capabilities, then, the other must find it unprofitable to shift resources from production to military preparation and raiding.[7] Clearly, this condition is implausible. We therefore conclude that the attainment of the first best as an equilibrium is unlikely.

REPEATED PLAY

We now focus on the choices that will be made when there is repeated play (as is likely in kinship societies).

Turning to the infinitely repeated version of the one-period game, we ask: When would the threat of reversion to the anarchy equilibrium deter raiding? When, that is, will $w_i = w', m_i = m', l_i = l', r_i = r' = 0$ for all i be supported on the equilibrium path of play?

To address this question, consider the following strategy: each player allocates resources according to $w_i = w', m_i = m', l_i = l'$ and does not raid[8] as long as the other player has allocated resources in the above manner and never raided. Otherwise, each player reverts to playing the strategy that yields what we call an anarchy equilibrium.[9] In this

---

[7] Further exploration reemphasizes the implausibility of attaining the first best as an SPE. The condition is fragile. It is less likely to exist the lower is the fixed cost in raiding; the higher is the total product, $F(w^*)$; and the lower is the marginal productivity of working, $\partial F(w^*)/\partial w_i$. If development implies better transportation technology, greater total production, and decreasing marginal returns to labor, then as development proceeds, the equilibrium will break down.

[8] That is, $r_i = r' = 0$.

[9] We signify the anarchy equilibrium by the subscript "a." In it, private agents, behaving rationally, devote efforts to military preparedness, even though it is costly and reduces the social welfare. We employ the anarchy equilibrium in future models to generate payoffs when players deviate from the equilibrium path of play.

equilibrium, private agents, behaving rationally, devote efforts to military preparedness, even though it is costly and reduces the social welfare.

On the path of play, each player's payoff is given by $\pi' = U(F(w'), l')$. π^D_1 is given by solving player 1's optimization problem, given that $w_2 = w', m_2 = m', l_2 = l'$. Player 2 can deviate in the first stage; he can also adhere to the equilibrium strategy in the first stage, thereby inducing player 1 to follow the equilibrium strategy in the second stage, and then deviate by raiding. Player 2's best deviation π^D_2 is thus given by $\max\{\pi, U\left(F(w') + F(w')M(m', m') - k, l'\right)\}$, where π is the solution to player 2's optimization problem (2), given that $w_1 = w', m_2 = m', l_1 = l'$.

A necessary and sufficient condition for the above strategy combination to be SPE is that $\forall I$, $\pi_i/(1 - \delta) \geq \pi^D_i + \pi^N_i/(1 - \delta)$.

THE IRRELEVANCE OF THE FOLK THEOREM

According to the folk theorem, the first best outcome can be attained in equilibrium in repeated play. For this to take place, the players' discount factor, δ, must be close to 1. Even were one to lack means of defense, that is, the other would not raid out of a fear reversion to the anarchy equilibrium. In addition, each player's discount rate and her beliefs about the discount rate of the other must be common knowledge.

Given these requirements, we discount the possibility of securing the first best through repeated play and focus instead on two other equilibria: a no-military (NM) equilibrium in which no one invests in military capabilities, m'1 = m'2 = 0; and a positive military (PM) equilibrium in which both players acquire military capabilities and m'1 = m'2 > 0.

The No-Military (NM) Equilibrium

In the NM equilibrium (in which m' = 0, then M(m', m') = 0), the payoffs for deviating can be simplified to

$$\pi^D_1 = \max_{w, m, I \geq 0, \; w+m+l=T} U(F(w) + R_1(w, w', m, 0)\left(F(w')M(m, 0) - k, l\right),$$

$$\pi^D_1 = \max_{w, m, I \geq 0, \; w+m+l=T} U(F(w) + R_2(w', w, 0, m', 0)\left(F(w')M(0, m) - k, l\right).$$

Because the NM investment equilibrium is a subset of the PM investment equilibrium,[10] the former cannot Pareto dominate the latter. But can the PM investment equilibrium Pareto dominate the NM investment equilibrium? If it can, we then learn that in societies without states, people may choose to live violently in order to increase their welfare.

THE POSITIVE MILITARY(PM) EQUILIBRIUM

Consider first a situation in which the one-time payoffs to defection are sufficiently high and the discount factor sufficiently low that future punishments fail to deter aggression. In such a case, for peace to prevail without investment in military ability, the players' allocation of resources between production and leisure must be such as to reduce the gains from raiding. The players must choose a level of productive effort, w^i, low enough to forestall raiding. More generally, in the most efficient NM investment equilibrium, each player deters the other from raiding by threatening to revert to the anarchy equilibrium and by making herself or himself poor enough so that raiding is not profitable. The price of peace is poverty.

Further analysis suggests that in societies without states, a seemingly wasteful investment in military ability can lead to an outcome that Pareto dominates the most efficient NM investment equilibrium. In the NM equilibrium, the amount of effort devoted to work is constrained by the need to reduce the productivity of the other player's raids; the parties devote residual resources to leisure rather than to labor. In the PM equilibrium, however, because the players devote more resources to deterring raiding, they can devote more resources to productive activity as well. An equilibrium in which the players make investments in military capabilities can therefore dominate an equilibrium in which no resources are devoted to military activity.[11]

In societies without states, then, the price of prosperity is the cost of preparing for war.

---

[10] Note that the no-military (NM) equilibrium is a special case of the positive military (PM) equilibrium, one in which $w' = 0$.

[11] It can do so when a redistribution of effort in the former equilibrium from leisure to work and military preparedness yields an increase in economic output that compensates for the loss of leisure, while still being low enough to ensure that raiding (which entails a reversion to the anarchy equilibrium) remains unprofitable.

An Impossibility Result?

CONCLUSION

The two figures below highlight the implications of this argument. Both portray the level of prosperity (on the *x* axis) and the level of security (on the *y*). The levels of each increase with the distance from the origin.

As depicted in Figure 3.1, in kinship societies there are two possible outcomes: one in which there is a high level of prosperity and a low level of security and another in which there is a high level of security but a low level of prosperity. As indicated by the arrows in Figure 3.2, people would prefer to have more of both. They would prefer, that is, to attain outcomes that reside in the upper right-hand corner of the diagram.[12] The dark line

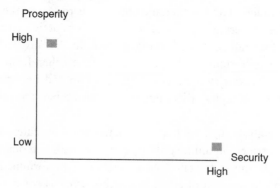

FIGURE 3.1 Possible outcomes

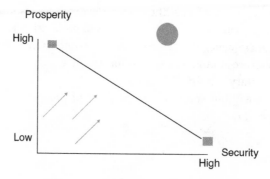

FIGURE 3.2 Preferences over outcomes

---

[12] Wherein is located the point at which the outcomes generate the maximum amount of utility.

running across the second figure indicates that when governed by kin, people are constrained from attaining such an outcome. We have argued that they are constrained by their institutions.

As we shall see when we return to the historical record, people respond to this situation with widespread demands for institutional changes – demands, that is, for the formation of states.

4

From Kinship to the State

Thus far we have focused on societies in which private families control the means of violence and made use of case materials drawn from the developing world. In this, the fourth chapter, we turn to history. Focusing primarily on Europe, we explore the formation of states.

Following the fall of the Roman and Carolingian empires, political order in Medieval Europe collapsed.[1] In the midst of disorder, people sought ways to assure their safety. So great was the level and so common the occurrence of violence that people traded labor for protection. Some, such as Bloch, call this the age of feudalism.[2] Others call it the "dark" ages. Not until the thirteenth century did Europe's economy begin to recover.

Central to Europe's recovery was the growth of the textile industry. On the one hand, it forged "forward linkages" with bankers, shippers, and merchants; on the other, it brought prosperity to the countryside as farmers began to invest in livestock and pasture lands and so supply the growing demand for wool. As might be expected, given the previous chapter, the increase in Europe's economic prosperity was accompanied by an increase in political disorder.

Drawn from Robert Bates, Avner Greif, and Smita Singh, 2002, "Organizing Violence." *Journal of Conflict Resolution* 46(5), 611–628.

[1] Harold Berman, 2003, *Law and Revolution*. Cambridge MA: Harvard University Press; Georges Duby, 1987, *France in the Middle Ages, 987–1460*. Oxford: Oxford University Press.

[2] Marc Bloch, 1970, *Feudal Society*. Chicago: University of Chicago Press. See also Daron Acemoglu and James A. Robinson, 2019, *The Narrow Corridor*. New York: Penguin Press; and Frances Fukuyama, 2011, *The Origins of Political Order*. New York: Farrar, Straus and Giroux.

Given the demand for wool, land became valuable and rural magnates, seeking to vest their rights in property, recruited "influential men into [their] following"[3] and soldiers who bore their colors. Rural Europe may have become more prosperous then. But it also became more violent, entering the period that McFarlane and others have called the era of "bastard feudalism."[4]

Not only lords and magnates but also common folk protested. Rallying in town squares, gathering in market places, and marching in the roads, they formed "peace movements." Religious leaders approached their monarchs and intimated that they, the monarchs, had been chosen by God and that He now charged them with defending those whom they ruled.[5]

In response to these appeals, monarchs appointed sheriffs, hired bailiffs, and recruited magistrates. In England, the magnates backed the reforms of Henry II, who banned private revenge and blood feuds. Such acts "were now treated as crimes against the common weal."[6] No longer subject to compensation or revenge, acts of violence were now subject to official proceedings.

In England and elsewhere in Europe, the political order thus changed. From the disorder of the Medieval period there emerged forces that tempered the use of violence. Rulers forged a political apparatus capable of apprehending, trying, and punishing those who infringed upon the welfare of others. The use of violence was now legitimate only if initiated by the state. It was the creation of states that made it possible to be both prosperous and secure; that made it possible, that is, to develop.

FORMALIZING THE ARGUMENT

To comprehend the processes that gave rise to this transformation, we return to the model set out in the previous chapter and introduce a new figure, G.[7] To finance his activities, G either raids the wealth of others or

---

[3] David Crouch, 1990, *William Marshall*. New York: Longman, p. 4.

[4] See K. B. McFarlane, 1973, *The Nobility of Later Medieval Europe*. Oxford: Clarendon, and *England in the 15th Century*. London: Hambledon; Michael Hicks, 1995, *Bastard Feudalism*. London: Longman.

[5] Thomas Head and R. Landes, 1992, *The Peace of God*. Ithaca: Cornell University Press. As for those who wished to continue to pillage and fight, the clerics announced, they should leave Europe, join the crusades, and take on the Slavs to the North or the Saracens to the East. See the famous speech by Pope Urban II at the Council of Clermont.

[6] Hicks, *Bastard Feudalism*, p. 113.

[7] "We" being Avner Greif, Smita Singh, and I. G can of course be thought of as a government.

secures the payment of taxes.[8] Agent i's net income, $I_i(\bullet)$, now includes revenue from productive labor and raiding minus taxes, if she chooses to pay; minus the expected reduction in her income resulting from predation by G.

G's objective is to maximize the value of her revenues from taxes and expropriation, discounted for time by a factor, δ_G. Given that private agents are themselves capable of violence, when G preys on the economic output of a player i, she succeeds only in a probability. This probability, q_i, reflects player i's ability to resist G, using her military power, m_i. Predation is costly and requires G to expend $CG > 0$ for each agent upon which she preys.

G's payoffs are given by $\sum \{p_i q_i \hat{I}_i (1 - \tau t_i) - Cp_i + \tau t_i \hat{I}_i\}$. The first term represents G's revenue from expropriating private agents' wealth, if G decides to engage in predation; the second, the costs of predation; and the third, G's income from taxation.

Using this framework, we can now specify the conditions under which a specialist in the use of violence, G, would refrain from predation and instead employ his power to protect the generation of wealth and in which the citizens would refrain from violence, engage in productive labor, enjoy their leisure, and pay taxes. When these choices persist in equilibrium, we can speak of a cooperative governance (CG) equilibrium, where the specialist in violence behaves as a government. The conditions that define this equilibrium characterize the state as well.

Analysis of the CG equilibrium suggests:

1. That the collection of taxes can induce G to use her coercive capabilities to protect property rights rather than to engage in predation.
2. That the equilibrium tax rate reflects not only the need to restrain predation by G but also to forestall a return to the private provision of violence.
3. And that the incentives for G to refrain from predation are a function of its prospective payoffs off the equilibrium path. These payoffs help determine whether a tax rate exists that private agents are willing to pay and that G finds sufficiently attractive to induce her to refrain from predation.

Further analysis suggests that political order will collapse following:

---

[8] Define $t_i \in \{0, 1\}$ to equal 1 if player i pays taxes and equal to 0 if she does not.

1. A lowering of the government's discount factor and a rise in its insecurity;
2. An increase in the prospects of the government off the equilibrium path;
3. A change in the relative military capabilities of government vis-à-vis private agents; or
4. A rise in productivity without an increase in taxation.

The derivation of these results appears in the Appendix to this chapter.

We now inspect more closely the incentives that govern the decision to remain on or to deviate from the equilibrium path of play – the conditions, that is, that underpin the formation of states.

ON THE EQUILIBRIUM PATH

G's incentives to adhere to the equilibrium path derive from the revenues the specialist in violence can secure from taxation. The tax rate, τ, that supports the cooperative governance (CG) equilibrium is limited from below by the need to induce G to refrain from predation. It needs to be high enough that G finds it optimal, given the private agents' strategies, to refrain from confiscating their wealth should they pay taxes.[9] On the other hand, it is bounded from above by the need to ensure that private agents will choose to pay taxes rather than withholding them.

If taxes are not fully paid, G must choose between punishing, thereby triggering a reversion to the warlord equilibrium, or refraining from doing so and remaining in the cooperative governance equilibrium. If the level of taxes is high, then the receipt of a portion of what is due might remain preferable to the payoffs under the warlord equilibrium. For G's threat to be credible, the level of taxation must therefore not be too high.

The tax rate is therefore bounded from both above and below and the conditions under which states can exist are constrained accordingly.[10]

Development, I have argued, implies the pursuit of prosperity and the safeguarding of life and property. Under the cooperative governance (CG) equilibrium, those who specialize in the use of violence strive to do both. They behave in ways that render the use of power developmental.

---

[9] It must be sufficiently high, that is, to induce G to enforce rather than violate property rights.

[10] For further details, turn to the Appendix.

STATE FAILURE

But what if the conditions that underpin this equilibrium fail to hold? The cooperative governance (CG) equilibrium gives way to the warlord (WL) equilibrium and the players revert to the use of strategies that impoverish the polity and endanger its inhabitants. In the words of Chinua Achebe, "things fall apart."[11]

Under this equilibrium, private agents raid, when it is profitable to do so; the specialist in violence, G, acting like a warlord, engages in predatory behavior; and people cease paying taxes.

When players shift from the cooperative governance to the warlord equilibrium, they devote more resources to military preparedness and leisure as they seek to respond and to deter predation by fellow citizens – and by the specialist in violence, now on the prowl. Productive efforts therefore decline, resulting in less output.

Whereas the steady flow of tax payments provides a positive check to the predatory behavior of the specialist in violence, the threat of reversion to the chaos of statelessness provides a negative one.[12] The threat of reversion to warlordism keeps both the government and citizens on the equilibrium path and G's continuation value, π_G^{WL}, therefore constitutes a critical parameter in the model.

Comparative Statics

The comparative statics of the model yield insights into the impact of other forces. The most relevant include:[13]

The government's discount factor: Should the its discount factor fall, the government would more heavily discount future punishments, rendering more alluring the payoffs from opportunistic defection.

The government's military advantage: Should the government's ability to extract income from private agents rise, the incentives for it to uphold its end of the governance bargain will weaken unless compensated by an increase in the tax rate and greater public revenues.

---

[11] Chinua Achebe, 1958, *When Things Fall Apart*. London: Heinemann.

[12] If π^{GWL} is too high, the taxes needed to induce G to behave as a government may also be so high as to make governance unattractive.

[13] Each derivation presumes that the most efficient CG equilibrium prevails. For further details, refer to Bates, Greif, and Singh, "Organizing Violence," pp. 611–628.

The technology of production: Were the productivity of labor to increase, a smaller rate of taxation would be required to maintain a cooperative governance equilibrium.

The government's prospects under warlordism: The more favorable the government's prospects as a warlord, the greater the amount that must be paid to keep it from predating.

Unfortunately we lack data by which to properly test most of these predictions. Qualitative data can be brought to bear upon the first, however. The data are drawn from the "third wave," when authoritarian regimes turned democratic at the end of the twentieth century.

The Former Soviet Union

When, in 1991, Gorbachev legalized the formation of opposition parties and opened legislative and executive positions to electoral competition, Klebnikov reports, elite officials in the Communist party and the security services – specialists in violence – proclaimed a "period of emergency."[14] Because their future in office was no longer assured, they began looting state enterprises, firms that extracted natural resources, and the banking system. In response, others began to withhold resources from the state. By late 1991, one-third of the country's regions had stopped paying taxes to the center.[15] Shleifer and Triesman describe similar levels of nonpayment by firms. "Federal public finances" fell into "crisis," they write, with "tax collections [falling] from about 18 percent of GDP in 1989 to about 11 percent in 1996."[16]

Not only did people withhold resources from the state; they also began to provide their own defenses. In the spring of 1993, Boris Yeltsin declared that two-thirds of all commercial enterprises in Russia had links to organized crime.[17] Throughout the Russian Federation, republics began to declare themselves sovereign and to recruit their own military forces.

The collapse of the Soviet Union thus provides evidence to suggest that, in conformity with the predictions of the model, a foreshortening of a government's time horizons and an increase in its rate of discount can

---

[14] Paul Klebnikov, 2000, *Godfather of the Kremlin: Boris Berezovsky and the Looting of Russia.* New York: Harcourt Brace.

[15] Daniel Treisman, 1999, *After the Deluge: Regional Crisis and Political Consolidation in Russia.* Ann Arbor: University of Michigan Press.

[16] Andrei Shleifer and Daniel Triesman, 2000, *Without a Map: Political Tactics and Economic Reform in Russia.* Cambridge, MA: MIT Press, p. 89.

[17] Klebnikov, *Godfather of the Kremlin*, p. 29.

precipitate plunder and corruption, spurring a fiscal crisis and the break-down of the state.

State Failure in Africa

The reintroduction of party competition in late twentieth-century Africa also led to the predatory use of public power.[18] Consider, for example, Tanzania, long considered a model of political probity. In the late 1980s, TANU (the Tanganyika African National Union, the ruling party) became increasingly corrupt. Many whom I interviewed in Tanzania attributed this to changes in its "culture"; long the party of government, TANU now faced the prospect of losing office, and its officers used their power to accumulate assets before leaving office.[19] In Zambia, in the late 1980s, the United National Independence Party (UNIP), once the governing party, was also compelled to compete for political power. By way of preparation, its leaders created a "pension plan," forcing the government to divert funds from projects and public servants to party activists who now faced the possibility of losing power.[20]

More systematic is the evidence of Block, Ferree, and Singh, who document the existence, significance, and magnitude of "political business cycles" in African politics.[21] They find evidence of the largest cycles in countries that allow electoral competition and therefore possess governments that face the prospect of being expelled from power.

Major changes in the variables that mark a key condition of the cooperative governance equilibrium thus lead, as the model predicts, to an increase in predation by those who held power.

CONCLUSION

This chapter has explored the conditions under which those who possess power will employ it to defend those who generate prosperity. It has explored as well the conditions under which those who hold power will

[18] Robert H. Bates, 2008, *When Things Fell Apart*. New York: Cambridge University Press.
[19] Interviews 1992.
[20] Robert H. Bates and Paul Collier, 1991, "The case of Zambia," in R. H. Bates and A. O. Krueger, eds., *Political and Economic Interactions in Economic Policy Reform*. Blackwell.
[21] Steven Block, Karen Ferree, and Smita Singh, 2003, "Multiparty Competition, Founding Elections, and Political Business Cycles in Africa." *Journal of African Economies* 12(3), 444–468.

turn predatory. By doing so, it has probed the foundations of the state and the conditions that make development possible.

When founding a state, those who specialize in the use of violence create a central political hierarchy – one composed of revenue collectors, judges, policemen, and soldiers. Chapter 5 focuses on this apparatus, and the chapters that follow note forces, political and economic, that temper its powers, thereby rendering it, unwittingly perhaps, a source of development.

APPENDIX TO CHAPTER 4

The Cooperative Governance (CG) Equilibrium

We begin by considering the subgame perfect equilibrium of the one-period game, which we call the warlord (WL) equilibrium.[22] In the WL equilibrium, G predates if it is profitable to do so. In addition, the economic agents raid each other, if their wealth and military strength make predation profitable.

Subgame perfection implies that $\forall i p_i = 1\{I_i(1 - \tau t_i)q_i > C\}$; that is, $p_i = 1$ if it is profitable for G to predate on agent i. We therefore define functions such that $p_1 = P_1(w_1, w_2, m_1, m_2, r_1, r_2, t_1)$ and $p_2 = P_2(w_1, w_2, m_1, m_2, r_1, r_2, t_2)$. Substituting P_2 into $\check{I}_2$, above, we can then express $\check{I}_2$ as a function of the parameters w_1, w_2, m_1, m_2, t_2, r_1, r_2. Therefore, $r_1 = 1\{\check{I}_1(w_1, w_2, m_1, m_2, t_1, t_2, 1) > \check{I}_1(w_1, w_2, m_1, m_2, t_1, t_2, 0)\}$. Similarly, we can express $\check{I}_1$ as a function of w_1, w_2, m_1, m_2, t_1, t_2, r_1. It follows that $r_1 = 1\{\check{I}_1(w_1, w_2, m_1, m_2, t_1, t_2, 1) > \check{I}_1(w_1, w_2, m_1, m_2, t_1, t_2, 0)\}$, which we denote by $R_1(w_1, w_2, m_1, m_2, t_1, t_2)$. Player 2 raids if the conditions are such that $r_2 = 1$; player 1, if $r_1 = 1$. Given w_2, m_2, l_2, t_2, player 1 therefore solves:

$$\max_{w, m, l \geq 0,\, w+m+l = T,\, t \in \{0, 1\}} U\Big(\big(F(w) + R_1(w, w_2, m, m_2, t, t_2)$$

$$\big(F(w_2)M(m, m_2) - k\big)$$

$$-R_2\big(w, w_2, m, m_2, t_2, R_1()[F(w)$$

$$+R_1(w, w_2, m,\ m_2, t, t_2)$$

$$\big(F(w_2)M(m, m_2)k\big)$$

$$M(m_2, m)](1 - \tau t)$$

$$\big(1 - P_1\big(w, w_2, m, m_2, R_1(), R_2(), t\big)q_1\big), l\Big).$$

---

[22] This equilibrium plays a role in our model of state-like societies similar to that played by the anarchy equilibrium in our model of societies without states.

Likewise, given w_1, m_1, l_1, t_1, player 2 solves

$$\max_{w, m, l \geq 0,\, w+m+l = T,\, t \in \{0,1\}} U([F(w) - R_1(w_1, w, m_1, m, t_1, t)$$

$$\Big(F(w)M(m_1, m)\Big)$$

$$+ R_2\Big(w_1, w, m_1, m, t, R_1()\Big)[F(w_1)$$

$$+ R_1(w_1, w, m_1, m, t_1, t)$$

$$\Big(F(w)M(m_1, m) - k\Big)]M(m_1, m) - k)]\,]$$

$$(1 - \tau t)\Big(1 - P\big(w, w_1, m, m_1, R_2(), R_1(), t\big)q_2\Big), l)^{23}$$

Now consider an infinite version of the game as discussed and denote by δ_G the time discount factor of G. A cooperative governance (CG) equilibrium requires that each private agent select $w_i^{CG}, m_i^{CG}, l_i^{CG}$ optimally (given the strategies of other players), refrain from raiding, and pay taxes to G if the other agent has not raided and G has never seized the wealth of a private agent. Otherwise, the private agents "revolt," refuse to pay taxes, and revert to self-defense, playing the WL equilibrium strategy over subsequent periods.

For her part, G, in the CG equilibrium, refrains from predating as long as neither private agent launches raids or fails to pay taxes. If either agent raids or fails to pay her or his taxes, G then becomes predatory; it begins to behave as a warlord, seizing the wealth of the private agents.[24] Predation and violence are thus deterred by the threat of permanent reversion to the warlord equilibrium, which is characterized by predation and low levels of output, as private agents seek security by investing in military preparedness or by remaining poor.

Formally, consider the infinitely repeated version of this game. We seek the conditions under which $w_i = w^C, m_i = m^C, l_i = l^C, t_i = t^C = 1$, $r_i = r^C = 0, p_i = p^C = 0 \forall I \in \{1, 2\}$ can be sustained on the equilibrium path of play by the threat of a reversion to the WL equilibrium.

Denote by π^{WL}_i the payoff of the punishment (WL) equilibrium for each player $i \in \{1, 2, G\}$. Note that on the equilibrium path of play, players 1 and 2 receive a payoff of $\pi^C_1 = \pi^C_2 = U(F(w^C)(1 - \tau), l^C)$ in each period, whereas G receives a payoff of $\pi^C_G = 2\tau F(w^C)$.

The best possible deviation for player 1, π^D_1, is given by solving her or his optimization problem, given that $w_2 = w^C, m_2 = m^C, l_2 = l^C, t_2 = t^C$. Similar to the case without G, player 2 can raid at stage 3 after choosing her

---

[24] Considering a similar equilibrium in which G punishes an agent who raided or failed to pay tax without reverting to the warlord equilibrium does not change the analysis.

or his equilibrium allocation of resources at stage 1. Hence, for player 2, π^D_2 is given by $\max\{\sim\pi, U((F(w^C) + F(w^C)M(m^C, m^C) - k)(1 - \tau)(1 - P(w^C, w^C, m^C, m^C, 1, 0, 1)q_2), l^C)\}$, where $\sim\pi$ is the solution to player 2's optimization problem, given that $w_1 = w^C, m_1 = m^C, l_1 = l^C, t_1 = t^C$. Finally, G's best deviation is given by $\pi^D_G = \pi^C_G + \sum 1\{F(w^C)(1 - \tau)q_i > C\}(F(w^C)(1 - \tau)q_i - C)$.

For this strategy to be an equilibrium strategy, no player should be able to gain from deviating after any history, within a period or across periods. Hence, four conditions must hold:

1. No economic agent can gain by raiding or refusing to pay taxes. That is, $\forall i \in \{1, 2\}$, $\pi^C i/(1 - \delta) \geq \pi^D i + \delta\pi^{WL}i/(1 - \delta)$. This condition insures that an agent finds it optimal neither to raid nor to renege on tax payments.

2. No agent can gain by altering the allocation of his or her resources while still deterring the other from raiding. That is, for $I = 1, 2$ $(w_i^C, m_i^C, l_i^C) \in$ argmax $U(F(wi)(1 - \tau), li)$, subject to $w_i^C + m_i^C + l_i^C = T$ and $\pi^C_{-i}/(1-\delta) \geq \pi^D_{-i} + \delta\pi^{WL}_{-i}/(1-\delta)$.

3. G's threat to predate within the period in which a raid is conducted must be credible. It must be profitable for G, and the cost to G of punishing a player who raids must, in equilibrium, therefore be less than the gains from doing so. Denote by $w^D i$ and $m^D i$ player i's allocation of resources to work and military capacity in its optimal deviation (which takes into account that G will predate in response). G's threat is credible if for all i, $(F(w^D_i) + F(w^C)M(m^D_i, m^C) - k)q_i > C$.[25]

4. And G finds must it optimal not to predate if the economic agents adhered to their strategies. That is, $\pi^C_g/(1-\delta) \geq \pi^D_g + \delta\pi^{WL}_g/(1-\delta)$.

[25] Note that this assumes that an economic agent's optimal deviation implies not paying tax.

5

Restraining the Leviathan: Part I

Development is marked by prosperity and security. As we have seen, if control over the means of violence remains in private hands, then there can be no development; to be prosperous, one must be prepared to fight. While the creation of a centralized political hierarchy may be necessary for the achievement of prosperity and security, clearly that cannot be sufficient, for those who preside over that hierarchy will themselves be tempted to employ their power to seize the wealth and imperil the well-being of others. To fully comprehend the political foundations of development, then, we need to explore how the power of centralized political institutions can be rendered a source of security rather than a source of danger. We need to probe the incentives that shape the behavior of the bureaucratic institutions that lie at the core of the state.

BUREAUCRACIES

When kinship polities transform into states, the transition is marked by the creation of bureaucracies. As detailed in the literature,[1] bureaucracies are

First published as David Soskice, Robert H. Bates, and David Epstein, "Ambition and Constraint: The Stabilizing Role of Institution." *Journal of Law, Economics and Organizations* 8(3) (October 1992), 547–560.
[1] Shmuel N. Eisenstadt, 1968, "Social Institutions: The Concept," in D. L. Sills, ed., *International Encyclopedia of the Social Sciences*. New York: MacMillan; Thomas Ford Hault, 1969, *Dictionary of Modern Sociology*. Totowa, NJ: Littlefield, Adams; and Samuel P. Huntington, 1968, *Political Order in Changing Societies*. New Haven: Yale University Press.

(1) Marked by a division of labor.
(2) Longer lived than their members. They contain persons of different generations.
(3) Hierarchical. They contain, that is, both senior and junior members, with juniors desiring to attain senior rank.
(4) Rule governed.

When politicians preside over institutions that exhibit these properties, I argue,[2] they tend to use the power of these institutions to nurture rather than plunder the wealth of their people. They render the polity "developmental."[3]

Leaders and Deputies

To formalize the argument, we introduce a leader $L[t]$ and a deputy $D[t]$. These actors appear as overlapping generations. As shown in Figure 5.1, each lives two periods, with the deputy, $D[t-1]$, becoming a leader at time t.

Each possesses a distinctive control variable: In each period t, the leader, $L[t]$, chooses a tax rate $a[t]$,[4] while the deputy chooses the amount of effort that she devotes to implementing or enforcing the policies of the leader. The level of (costless) effort, $e[t]$, can be set to 0 or 1. If the deputy chooses $e = 0$, then she fails to implement the leader's choice of policy; if she chooses $e = 1$, she perfectly implements L's policy.

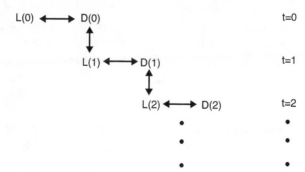

FIGURE 5.1 Deputies from one period become leaders in the next.

[2] David Soskice, David Epstein, and I.
[3] Scholars have long noted that people who live in states are more prosperous than those who live in kinship polities. Using data on the heights exhibited by human remains, Carles Boix, for example, recently published a study that reports that people who lived in state-like polities were taller and better nourished than those who did not. See Carles Boix, 2015, *Political Order and Inequality*. New York: Cambridge University Press.
[4] Where $a[t]$ lies in the closed interval $[0, 1]$.

The actors possess distinctive preferences. The leader seeks to maximize the public revenue, equal to the tax rate ($a[t]$) applied to the national income $y[t]$, or $a[t]\,y[t]$, where national income is derived solely from investments made in the previous period.

Investment is made in period $t-1$ and is assumed to depreciate fully in period t. It therefore has no effect on national income after time t. Accordingly, we set $y[t] = y(I[t-1])$, where $I[t]$ stands for the quantity of investment made in period t.

The deputy possesses political ambition, as captured in parameter b that lies in the half-open interval [0, 1). The deputy wants to become a leader. As a consequence, the deputy's objective function can be written as

$$U(D[t]) = ba[t]y[t]e[t] + (a[t+1]y[t+1]e[t+1])/[1+r].$$

The second term in $U(D[t])$ indicates the benefits a deputy will enjoy in period $t+1$ (i.e., when she becomes a leader). These benefits depend on the tax rate she sets in the period, $a[t+1]$; the national income in time $t+1$, which is determined by the level of investment in time t; and the cooperation of future deputies in implementing the tax rate, $e[t+1]$ – all discounted by $[1+r]$.

The first term indicates the satisfaction the deputy enjoys while still a deputy. The level of satisfaction depends upon the financial rewards of being a political leader, $a[t]\,y[t]\,e[t]$, *discounted* by b (i.e., by having to be enjoyed while not yet attaining the status of leader). The *more* ambitious the deputy, the *smaller* the level of b.[5] The implication, of course, is that if political advancement is rule bound, then the deputy can be induced to obey and enforce the rules so as to satisfy her political ambition.

Lurking off stage, as it were, is a third set of actors: a "cloud" of investors. They are large in number; being atomistic, they can neither coordinate nor play strategically.[6] They choose $I[t-1]$ (or investment at time $t-1$) to maximize their expected net benefits:

$$y[t](1 - a[t]e[t]) - [1+r]I[t-1].$$

---

[5] Deputies with b = 0 care only about their rewards while being a leader in the following period and not at all about their present payoffs.

[6] It should be noted that, given the sequence of play (see Figure 5.2), the results would hold even were investors able to behave strategically. The results do not depend upon the threat of investors to defect. Investor threats to dis-invest or to move their capital elsewhere cannot influence the leader's payoffs in period t; their investments bear fruit only in period $t+1$. Nor would such threats influence the deputy's decision in period $t+1$; investors have already invested in the previous period.

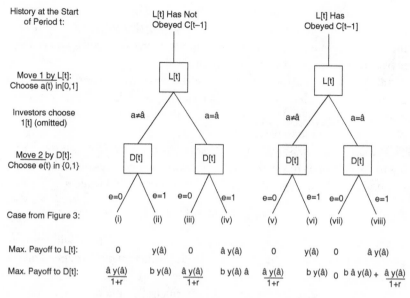

FIGURE 5.2 The game tree

Because investors do not behave strategically, their behavior is not modeled explicitly in the game (see Figure 5.2).

The Rules

Institutions are rule governed. In this instance, the rules are:

[1] $a[t] = \hat{a}$;

[2] $e[t] = 0$, if $L[t]$ has broken the constitution $(C[t])$,
$e[t] = 1$, otherwise;

[3] $L[t]$ has broken the rules if $L[t]$ fails to carry out $C[1]$ in the present period or has failed to carry out $C[2]$ in the previous period.

The first clause commits the leader to a particular choice of tax rate: $\hat{a}$ stands for the mandated rate of taxation.[7] The second commits the deputies to render the leader's choice of policies ineffective if the leader

---

[7] Note that, although C requires adopting a constant tax rate, it could be easily amended to specify a variable tax rate, as long as the variation was dependent only on factors that are commonly observable. In addition, since deputies possess the power to collect taxes, it is realistic to assume that they would also possess the power to extort bribes. As in the case of a nonconstant tax rate, our model can accommodate this situation as long as there is a regular bribe schedule that all deputies follow and that is known in advance to the investors.

breaks the rules. The third clause defines what is meant by breaking the rules; C[1] refers to the first clause, C[2] to the second. By this third clause, an official breaks the rules either by failing to preserve the agreed-upon tax rate when a leader or, when a deputy, by failing to punish a leader who has altered the tax rate.

The strategy of "obeying the rules" can therefore be defined as follows:

$D[t]$ follows C[2] in period t and then C[1] in period $t + 1$; if $D[t]$ does not follow C[2] as a deputy, she sets $a[t + 1] = 1$ upon becoming a leader.

By this strategy, an official, when a "good" deputy, will punish a leader who alters the agreed-upon tax rate (but effectively implement the policies of a leader who keeps to the promised tax rate); and, while a leader, will preserve the tax rate. When "bad," the official will, while a deputy, leave a bad leader unpunished and, while a leader, set the tax rate to 1.

By the logic that characterizes the bureaucracy, those who inhabit it, if ambitious, will obey its rules and employ its power to grow, rather than despoil, the economy.[8]

A STABLE COMMITMENT?

The central questions become: Given its characteristics, can a political hierarchy induce restraint? Can it induce restraint among those who occupy its ranks and exercise its power? Will those empowered by it refrain from using their power to engage in predation?

The answer to each question is "yes." In this section, we show that there exists a tax rate $\hat{a}$ at which "obeying the rules" is a subgame

---

[8] Before proceeding, we note several additional assumptions. We assume that there is perfect information, in the sense that the rules of the game and the payoffs for the players are common knowledge; that at each move the relevant player knows the full history of the game; and that investors possess perfect foresight or rational expectations and, at $t - 1$, are able to solve the game between successive generations of politicians for $a[t]$. We assume that the polity cannot transfer tax revenues between time periods nor carry out public investments. We also assume that there is no labor and that capital depreciates fully in one period. $Y[t]$ therefore depends solely on private investment in the previous period, $I[t - 1]$. The opportunity cost of the investment is r, which can be thought of as the return to investing in other countries, and which for convenience we set equal to the discount rate of the deputies. Thus $a[t]$ determines the level of current income for investors as $y[t] (1 - a[t] e [t])$; net profits are $y[t] (1 - a[t] e[t]) - I[t - 1] [1 + r]$. Note that $a[t]$ also determines political current public revenues, equal to $a[t] y[t] e[t]$.

perfect equilibrium (SGPE) choice of strategy for both leaders and deputies.[9]

Theorem 1 registers this claim.

Theorem 1. *If for all t, D[t] follows s*(â), s*(â) is a subgame perfect strategy combination if â/[1 + r] > b.*

Proof: At the start of any period, there are only two relevant histories: that in which $L[t]$ obeyed $C[t-1]$ while a deputy and that in which she did not. In Figure 5.2, the first history is represented by the right game tree, the second by the left.

Informally, consider the two possible sets of end points: those when $D[t]$ has obeyed the rules and those when $D[t]$ has not. We can enter those end points into two payoff tables (Figure 5.3) and identify the payoffs at each end point (Figure 5.4).

For s^* to be a subgame perfect equilibrium (SGPE) strategy, if the game strays off the equilibrium path, $D[t]$ must be willing to implement her punishment strategy. That is, in the left-hand table of Figure 5.4, the deputy must prefer to obey C by punishing $L[t]$ no matter which action she takes. The conditions for this are $D_3 > D_4$ and $D_1 > D_2$. In addition, if the game is on the equilibrium path, then the players must be willing to continue to obey the rules. This means that the deputy would rather set $e = 1$ if the leader obeys C and $e = 0$ if the leader violates C, and that the leader would rather obey C than not. These conditions imply $D_8 > D_7$, $D_5 > D_6$, and $L_8 > L_6$. Taken together, these conditions imply $â/[1 + r] > b$.[10]

An SGPE therefore exists. As is to be expected, it requires that the shadow of the future looms sufficiently large to constrain present behavior.

Theorem 1 demonstrates that obeying the rules constitutes a subgame perfect strategy, conditional on $â/[1 + r] > b$ (or on the discounted future returns of being a leader being greater than the level of ambition). Note that the outcome is stationary, since the tax rate will be consistent over time; hence, so too will investment and national income be consistent over time.

Theorem 2 defines more precisely the range of tax rates that possess this property and thereby yield stable commitments.

---

[9] That is, a tax rate that will not be changed.

[10] An algebraic proof is provided in the Appendix.

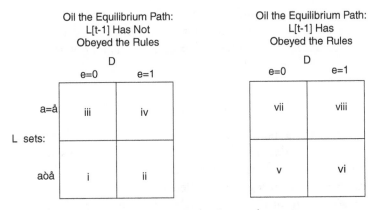

FIGURE 5.3 End points to the game

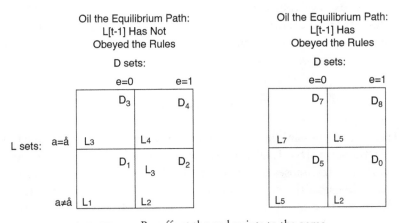

FIGURE 5.4 Payoffs at the end points to the game

Theorem 2. *No SGPE exists in which L[t] sets â such that â/[1 + r] < b along the equilibrium path.*

We offer the proof in the Appendix.

Theorems 1 and 2 set out the conditions under which the actors will maintain a commitment, one that will be will last for generations. Four major properties of the institution induce such behavior. The first is the existence of overlapping generations. The second is a division of labor, with mutual interdependence between generations. The third is hierarchy and the possibility, therefore, of ambition. And the last is rule governance.

These conditions are sufficient to make those ambitious for power willing to sacrifice economic consumption to secure political office, with the consequence that they obey a set of rules that provides a stable environment for investors.[11]

CONCLUSION

The life of the central political hierarchy exceeds the lives of its members and generations overlap, junior office holders seek to attain senior rank, there is a division of labor, and behavior is rule governed. Given these attributes, rather than being an instrument by which those with power can extract resources from those without, a central political hierarchy can instead provide stability for periods of long duration – durations that exceed the lifetimes of their members. They can "incentivize" those with power to exercise restraint.

Insofar as we capture the logic that governs behavior within the bureaucracies, we can better understand how states came to provide an environment in which development could take place.

PROOF OF THEOREM I

There are two possible histories to consider. First, $L[t]$ has not obeyed C: If $L[t]$ chooses $a[t] = 1$, $D[t]$ chooses $e[t] = 0$ if $a/[1 + r] > b$. If $L[t]$ chooses $a[t] = \hat{a}$, $D[t]$ chooses $e[t] = 0$ if $a/[1 + r] > b$. Second, $L[t]$ has obeyed C: If $L[t]$ chooses $a[t] = \hat{a}$, $D[t]$ chooses $e[t] = 1$. If $L[t]$ chooses $a[t] = 1$, $D[t]$ chooses $e[t] = 0$ if $\hat{a}/[1 + r] > b$. Therefore, for each history, $D[t]$ obeys C. In $t + 1$, $D[t]$, now $L[t + 1]$, again faces two histories. First, $D[t]$ has not obeyed C: Then, since $D[t + 1]$ sets $e[t] = 0$, whatever $D[t + 1]$ chooses, $L[t + 1]$ loses nothing by setting $a[t + 1] = 1$. Second, $D[t]$ has obeyed C: Then $D[t]$ chooses $a[t + 1] = \hat{a}$, gaining $\hat{a}y(\hat{a})/[1 + r]$ as opposed to 0 if $D[t]$ were to have chosen $a[t + 1] = 1$ (since $D[t + 1]$ chooses $e[t + 1] = 1$ in the first case and $e[t + 1] = 0$ in the second).
Therefore, for all possible histories, $D[t]$ will play $s^*(\hat{a})$, if $\hat{a}/[1 + r] > b$.
Q.E.D.

---

[11] It should be noted and stressed that we have established the existence of an equilibrium, not its uniqueness. Other equilibria can exist; in our model, as in other repeated games, the folk theorem applies.

PROOF OF THEOREM 2

Assume the contrary, so that $L(t)$'s payoff from setting $a[t] = a'$ is $a'y(a')$. It will pay L to set $a = a'$, rather than $a = 1$, if $a'y(a') > y(a')e$; this requires $D[t]$ to set $e = 0$ if $L[t]$ sets $a = 1$. There is no SGPE if the maximum gain $D[t]$ can be given by $D[t + 1]$ for setting $e = 0$ is less than the minimum payoff $D[t + 1]$ can restrict $D[t]$ to for setting $e[t] = 1$. If $e[t] = 1$, the minimum payoff is $by(a')$, achieved by $e[t + 1] = 0$. The maximum gain will be of the form $ay(a)$; this is because, as part of an SGPE, this will be known to investors, so that the $a[t]$ they take into account in their investment decision in t will be the same as $a[t + 1]$. Whatever this value of a, say a'', $D[t]$ (as $L[t + 1]$) must not have an incentive to set $a[t + 1] = 1 > a''$. Hence it must also be true for a'' that $by(a'') < a''y(a'')$. But for $a'' < b$, this is not the case. Therefore the maximum gain $R(\hat{a})$ requires $\hat{a} > b$. Now if $a^* < b$, $R(\hat{a}) < R(b) < R(a^*)$ for $\hat{a} > b$; and if $a^* < a'' < b$, $by(a'') > a''y(a'') = R(a'') > R(b) > R(\hat{a})$. Therefore, if $a^* < a' < b$, the minimum payoff to which D can be held, namely, $by(a')$, is greater than the maximum payoff that D can receive, $R(\hat{a})$.

Q.E.D.

6

Restraining the Leviathan: Part II

As argued previously, the bureaucratic core of the state – the central political hierarchy – not only empowers monarchs but also restrains them. In this chapter, we find that another factor constrains their use of power: their need for income. We demonstrate that a government's need to bargain grows as its tax base becomes more mobile. As financial markets increase in size and trade expands and as capital surpasses rents as the greatest source of income, then wealth can elude the grasp of the state. Because a government must now bargain with those who can pay its bills, the latter are now in a position to shape public policy.

To establish these claims, we return to history. And to test the inferences we draw from case materials, we again formalize our arguments.

WAR AND TAXES

Historians of Western Europe stress that the fiscal problems of those atop the central political hierarchy arose from the need to finance their wars. Noting that "the traditional revenues of the crown ... were quite inadequate for his needs [and that] the fines and scutages ... did not come near to raising the funds needed to pay troops," Michael Prestwich interprets the reign of Edward I in terms of his search for new sources of income.[1]

Originally published as Robert H. Bates and Da Hsiang Donald Lien, 1985, "A Note on Taxation, Development, and Representative Government," *Politics and Society* 14, 53–70.

[1.] Michael Prestwich, 1972, *War, Politics and Finance under Edward I*. London: Faber and Faber Limited, p. 18. See also J. G. Edwards, 1967, "The Personnel of the Commons in Parliament under Edward I and Edward II," in Andrew G. Little and Frederick M. Powicke, eds., *Essays in Medieval History Presented to Thomas Frederick Tout*,

And commenting on fourteenth-century France, John Bell Henneman states "the king had to pay his troops. Some military forces had to be maintained during truces or in times of peace ... Continually short of money, the king had to consider two possible remedies: one was the use of fiscal expedients which might provide a temporary windfall; the other was to find a different basis for taxation."[2] As Henneman bluntly states: "taxes were virtually synonymous with war financing."[3]

Warfare did not determine the nature of the tax system nor the political consequences of that choice, however. As Zolberg contends, when "the central power [looked] within the country for more efficient means of mobilizing the resources he needed, the effects produced were by no means exclusively determined by the external stimulus."[4] Rather, "it seems ... that ... a set of economic and social conditions dictated to the English state a strategy for mobilizing resources based primarily on trade whereas France, while developing the salt tax, lived mainly on direct taxes, and that this difference contributed to the differentiation of their representative institutions."[5]

The English monarchy sought to tax trade, and this, Zolberg argues, promoted the growth of parliamentary democracy, in which those atop the central political hierarchy were compelled to bargain with their subjects when seeking a share of their wealth. The question is: Why?

THE NATURE OF THE TAX BASE

One of the most striking features of the evidence is that it was the taxation of "moveable" property that promoted the conferral of political representation by revenue-seeking monarchs.

In England, traditional sources of revenue included collections from royal lands, taxes on the clergy, the proceeds of justice, and feudal aids. Such traditional taxes proved insufficient to meet the costs of warfare. As a consequence, Edward I introduced taxes on trade and on moveables.

Manchester: Books for Libraries Press, 197–214; Albert F. Pollard, 1926, *The Evolution of Parliament.* London: Longman, Green and Co.; and May McKisack, 1932, *The Parliamentary Representation of the English Boroughs during the Middle Ages.* London: Frank Cass.

[2.] John Bell Henneman, 1971, *Royal Taxation in Fourteenth Century France: The Development of War Financing, 1322–1356.* Princeton: Princeton University Press, p. 22.

[3.] Ibid., vii.

[4.] Aristide R. Zolberg, 1980, "Strategic Interactions and the Formation of Modern States: France and England." *International Social Science Journal* 32(4), 687–716, 695.

[5.] Ibid.

Moveables were assets that could be hidden; they were "cows, oxen, grain, household goods, and other possessions-property that could be transferred from place to place."[6]

The taxes on trade and moveables proved highly lucrative. Thus Sydney Knox Mitchell notes that, "properly administered, they yielded far more than any other levy that we have heard about before, approaching the fabulous sums raised under the Anglo-Saxons."[7] They possessed two significant shortcomings, however. They could be easily avoided. And partially as a consequence, they had to be bargained for.

In discussing the politics surrounding the introduction of the tax on the wool trade, Joseph R. Strayer notes both limitations:

> The experiment should have demonstrated two things to Edward's advisers. In the first place ... an increase of approximately 100% in the [tax] rate did not yield an increase of 100% in the returns. In the second place, it was clear that any attempt to secure increases ... by nonparliamentary means would cause serious protests.[8]

A similar pattern emerged in France. Thus Henneman also notes that the monarch's attempts to raise greater levels of taxes led to the creation of forms of political representation. As he states,

> A major purpose of [my] study is to relate the legal theories to actual practice, and in so doing we must look for guidance to the institutional historians. Their most valuable contributions have concerned representative institutions and the mechanisms of consent .... According to the maxim *quod omnes tangit*, those whose rights were affected had to consent .... On a more practical level, no tax could be collected without considerable cooperation from those who were taxed, so their acquiescence was needed .... If we are to understand the constitutional implications of taxation in this period, we must

---

[6.] James Field Willard, 1934, *Parliamentary Taxes on Personal Property 1290 to 1334: A Study in Medieval English Feudal Administration.* Cambridge, MA: The Medieval Academy of America, p. 3.

[7.] Sydney Knox Mitchell, 1951, *Taxation in Medieval England.* New Haven: Yale University Press, p. 6.

[8.] Joseph R. Strayer, 1947, "Introduction," in William A. Morris and Joseph R. Strayer, eds., *The English Government at Work, 1327–1336.* Cambridge, MA: The Medieval Academy of America, p. 8. Note also that Prestwich concludes: "Taxes on moveables had been developed into an essential financial expedient. The attempts to make use of taillage and a feudal aid in the last years of the reign had shown that there was little future in prerogative forms of taxation. It was clear that the consent and goodwill of the community of the realm was essential if adequate supplies of funds were to be forthcoming, and the importance of Edward's financial expedients in promoting a system of parliamentary representation is self evident." Prestwich, *War,* 222–223.

relate taxation to the use of assemblies and relate both to the question of consent.[9]

In common with many other historians of this period in French history – the mid-fourteenth century – Henneman analyzes the variety of political doctrines used to justify the levying of, or resistance to, taxation. But in the course of Henneman's narrative, it becomes increasingly clear that the "practical" considerations were more significant than the doctrinal. Communities living in or near war zones proved more willing to pay for defense than those who lived distant from them. Taxes on fixed assets, such as the *gabelle*, were set and levied without consent.[10] The more commercialized areas of France paid a sales tax; the less commercialized paid a hearth tax.[11] Taxes on towns were negotiated. And so too were taxes upon the wealthier, more commercialized sectors of the country.[12] The level of taxation and representation accorded to different areas. then, appears to have depended less upon the legal merits of various doctrines and more upon the political and economic factors that determined the level of demand for the monarch's protection and upon the capacity to evade the monarch's levies.

Several other features of the tax systems are notable. One was the evolution of corporate forms, a theme stressed in the writings of those who, like Henneman, Strayer, and Prestwich, are preoccupied with the rise of political representation. By corporate forms, these scholars appear to mean institutions in which a subset of similarly situated agents in the political economy could make agreements binding on all such agents. One reason for the evolution of such agencies, they stress, is that the bargaining for taxes was costly to monarchs. Monarchs therefore appear to have desired to bargain with fewer agents – ones representative of the set of all agents.[13] In addition to lower costs, the benefits of a collectively binding

---

[9.] Henneman, *Royal Taxation*, 25–26.   [10.] Ibid., 169.   [11.] Ibid., 166.

[12.] See also the important pieces, Margaret Levi, "Towards a Theory of Rule and Revenue Production: The Fiscal Basis of the Early Modern State of France and Britain" (manuscript, April 1983); and William Brustein and Margaret Levi, "Rulers, Rebels and Regions, 1500–1700" (Paper presented at the annual meetings of the Public Choice Society, Atlanta, March 1983). See also Joseph Schumpeter, 1954, "The Crisis of the Tax State," in A. Peacock, et al., ed., *International Economic Papers*. New York: Macmillan; and Otto Hintze, 1955, "The Formation of the State and Constitutional Development: A Study in History and Politics," in Felix Silbert, ed., *The Historical Essays of Otto Hintze*. New York: Oxford University Press.

[13.] Thus Henneman notes: "The brief memorandum submitted to the King in 1339 certainly suggests that the government would have preferred to negotiate taxes with assemblies rather than doing so locally." Henneman, *Royal Taxation*, 326.

agreement were greater than the benefits of a tax that was imposed on the agents singly. Given the mobility of assets, were any one asset holder to pay a tax while others did not, the tax yield would decline as the moveable assets shifted into the hands of those who remained untaxed. For these (and other) reasons, monarchs preferred collective, rather than individual levies.

Historical sources reveal that taxpayers themselves also preferred to negotiate collectively. Those acceding to a tax preferred that all similarly situated agents be taxed at the same rate. In France, for example, according to Henneman, "local jealousies led towns to make subsidy grants conditional upon similar grants from other towns,"[14] behavior that no doubt reflected the desire and ability of business to locate in the municipality paying lower taxes.

It should be noted that the dynamics outlined thus far help to explain the manner in which the incentives to "free-ride" were overborn. Once initiated, tax-setting institutions quickly became "universal"; they set rates for all similarly situated agents. It therefore became difficult to receive the benefits of public policy while evading the costs of taxes.

Considerations arising on both the side of the monarch, who sought taxes, and the asset bearers, who paid them, thus favored the evolution of collectively binding agreements, and such considerations were related to the mobility of taxables.[15] As Mitchell concludes,

The old individualism of the aid vanished and in its place appeared corporate action. The fruitfulness of the levies on moveables and hence the desire to draw all property under contribution and the inability or impracticability of consulting all property holders led to the employment of representatives that might act in behalf of the taxpayers.[16]

---

14. Ibid., 319.
15. The enforcement of agreements also imposed costs on monarchs. They therefore demanded that those with whom they negotiated be in a position to make commitments that were binding. Thus, again and again, scholars note that monarchs, in calling for representative assemblies, demanded that the delegates who were sent to negotiate taxes be fully empowered to make binding pledges. See, for example, Henneman, *Royal Taxation*, 167ff; Prestwich, *War*, 179ff; and Morris and Strayer, *The English Government*, passim.
16. Mitchell, *Taxation*, 163. The argument thus far covers the taxation of all similarly situated agents – all members of a common trade or occupation, and so on. Insofar as the spread and completion of markets led to the broader mobility of assets, then the span of the binding agreements could be expected to broaden. The movement of tax negotiations to the level of the great council in England (Mitchell, *Taxation*, 206ff) and the establishment of national tax rates as opposed to ones for locales (Willard, *Parliamentary Taxes*, 65ff) suggest the operation of such forces. Their slower operation in France suggests the slower

A FORMALIZATION OF THE ARGUMENT

This brief review of early taxation in Europe thus suggests:

That monarchs were driven to seek new taxes in order to finance wars;
That in their search for increased taxes they expanded their tax base to include trade and moveable property;
And that a variety of considerations, including the elasticity of the tax yield, made it necessary for them to bargain with those who possessed property rights over the moveable tax base and to share with them formal control over the conduct of public affairs.

To test this argument, we formalize it and determine whether its conclusions follow from its premises. We assume the existence of a monarch (actor "1") and a collection of taxpayers. Assuming, for the purposes of simplicity, that the taxpayers are similar in critical respects, we will label them actor "2".[17] The monarch desires revenues and prefers some policies over others. The monarch's most preferred policy we label V^+. The more revenues he possesses and the closer his government's policy position (V) to his ideal point, the greater his satisfaction. We assume the monarch to be rational; he therefore chooses the tax rate, t, and policy position, V, that maximize his utility (u^1).

The monarch is not an autonomous agent, however; he depends for his taxes upon the citizens. It is citizens who control the tax base. The citizens desire money, which they derive from the after-tax profits of their enterprises, and favor certain policies; we label their most preferred policy position V^-. The greater their after-tax incomes, and the more government policies approximate their policy preferences, the more satisfied they are. Given the monarch's choice of a tax rate and government policy position, and given market prices for inputs and products, the citizens then choose the levels of capital (K) and labor (L) that maximize their utility (u^2).

We assume that at the outset the monarch's and citizens' choices rest in political-economic equilibrium. The problem then is: given an exogenous shock, such as a war, that leads to a need for greater taxes, and given the monarch's desire to remain in political-economic equilibrium (so that u^2 remain $\geq \bar{u}^2$), how are taxes likely to be raised?

The problem we are analyzing takes the form of a game. There are two maximizing agents, a monarch and the citizenry. At one level, their goals conflict; they conflict over policy and over the apportionment of the

---

evolution of national markets there. See also David Friedman, 1977, "A Theory of the Size and Shape of Nations." *Journal of Political Economy* 85 (February), 59–77.

[17.] A major difference between this model in and that in other Chapters in this volume is that economic agents here can choose strategically.

national product between the private sector and the fiscal. But at another level, the two depend upon each other. The government determines policies, which the citizens care about; and the citizens determine the magnitude of the national product, which constitutes the monarch's tax base.

The model can be outlined as follows:

The monarch's problem:

$$\max_{(t,V)} u^1 = u^1\left((t)f(K,L), -(V-V^+)^2\right)$$

such that $u^2 \geq u^{-2}$.

The citizenry's problem:

$$\max_{(K,L)} u^2 = u^2\left((1-t)f(K,L) - rK - wL, -(V-V^+)^2\right)$$

where:

$V \, \varepsilon \, [V^-, V^+]$

and

u^1 = the utility of the monarch

u^2 = the utility of the citizens

u^{-2} = the ability of the citizens at the moment of political-economic equilibrium

V = the policy of the government

V^+ = the monarch's preferred policy position

V^- = the citizens' preferred policy position

K = capital

L = Labor

r = the price of capital

w = the price of labor

$f(K, L)$ = the output generated from capital and labor.

Let η stand for the elasticity of supply of a given industry. It can be assumed that the more mobile the factors of production employed in the industry, the greater the elasticity of the production of output from that industry. When choosing an optimum tax rate, one that maximizes his utility, the monarch will then choose a t that possesses the following property (see Appendix):

$$\frac{\partial t}{\partial \eta} < 0.$$

That is, *the monarch will impose higher taxes on those sectors of the economy that are less elastic, that is, those that possess the less-mobile factors of production.*

But within the set of optimal taxes we also find that (see Appendix):

$$\frac{\partial(V - V^-)}{\partial t} < 0$$

and

$$\frac{\partial^2(V - V^-)}{\partial t \partial \eta} < 0.$$

That is, to maximize his utility, the monarch, behaving rationally, will trade off concessions in policies for increases in the tax rate. Moreover, the monarch will do this to a greater degree the higher the elasticity of the tax base. The implication of both findings is clear: *Those sectors that possess more mobile factors will have greater control over public policy.*[18]

SOME WISE MEN

It is interesting to turn to the writings of others who have thought about the linkages between taxation and representation in historical Europe. Among them would be Montesquieu; the physiocratic writers, Quesney and Mirabeau; and Albert Hirschman, whose work has done so much to revive the interest of contemporary political economists in these earlier writers and whose noted essay, *Exit, Voice and Loyalty* arrives at conclusions strikingly at variance with our own.

[18.] As can be seen in the specification of the model, the validity of these assertions depends upon the assumption of private rights in property. In this connection, it is notable that medieval monarchs clearly did not confer influence over policy to foreigners, such as Italians or Jews. Being foreigners, these groups lacked secure property rights and thus the "leverage" achieved by other groups who controlled taxable assets.

In constructing the model, we have represented the preferences of the monarch as diverging from those of the taxpayer; in this way, we have been able to explore the impact of bargaining. Were the case degenerate – that is, were V^+ precisely equal to V^- – then the monarch would simply become an agent of the private interests for purposes of policy making. The model would then represent the classic instrumentalist-Marxist theory of the state, and taxation would represent the financing of a government that supplies policies embodying the interests of the privileged classes.

MONTESQUIEU

As Hirschman's review of Montesquieu in his *The Passions and the Interests* suggests, Montesquieu was convinced that the rise of commerce generated desirable political consequences. As Montesquieu wrote, "it is almost a general rule that wherever the ways of men are gentle . . . there is commerce; and wherever there is commerce, the ways of men are gentle."[19] Commerce, Montesquieu held, promotes the reduction of the arbitrary use of state power. In particular, the increased mobility of assets, Montesquieu argued, engendered restraint on the part of monarchs. Writing of the invention of the letter of credit, Montesquieu stated, "through this means commerce could elude violence . . . ; for the richest trader had only invisible wealth which could be sent everywhere without leaving any trace . . . . Since that time, the rulers have been compelled to govern with greater wisdom than they themselves have intended."[20]

QUESNAY AND MIRABEAU

In their *Philosophie Rurale*, the physiocrats, Quesnay and Mirabeau, also commented on the political consequences of the rise of commerce. Their conclusion bears a strong similarity to our own:

All the possessions [of commercial societies] consist . . . of scattered and secret securities, a few warehouses, and passive and active debts, whose true owners are to some extent unknown, since no one knows which of them are paid and which of them are owing. No wealth which is immaterial is kept in people's pockets can ever be got hold of by the sovereign power, and consequently will yield it nothing at all . . . . The wealthy merchant, trader, banker, etc., will always be a member of a republic. In whatever place he may live, he will always enjoy the immunity which is inherent in the scattered and unknown character of his property . . . . It would be useless for the authorities to try to force him to fulfill the duties of a subject: they are obliged, in order to induce him to fit in with their plans, to treat him as master, and to make it worth his while to contribute voluntarily to the public revenue.[21]

ALBERT HIRSCHMAN

It is from Hirschman's writings that the above quotations are drawn. But what of his own theorizing?

[19.] Quoted in Albert O. Hirschman, 1977, *The Passions and the Interests: Political Arguments for Capitalism before Its Triumph*. Princeton: Princeton University Press, p. 60.
[20.] Ibid., 72–73.   [21.] Ibid., 94–95.

In the model he presents in *Exit, Voice and Loyalty*, Hirschman argues that an asset owner under adverse economic conditions possesses two alternatives: to exit from the market or to "give voice," that is, to remain in the market but to alter conditions within it through political action.[22] One reason for remaining in the market is loyalty; loyal consumers of "widgets," for example, will purchase them even in periods of declining quality while lobbying the management to rectify defects. Another is the cost of mobility. Given high opportunity costs of switching, the product may be inelastically consumed, even in periods of declining quality, or inelastically supplied, even while facing declining prices. Workers, for example, may be too old to leave a declining industry, or skills and capital may be too specialized to switch to the production of other commodities.

By Hirschman's reasoning, then, we should predict that the owners of immobile factors will take the political initiative; they will give voice and express their preferences in arenas other than the market. Our model predicts the opposite.

There are two basic reasons for the contrasting results. One is that we allow tradeoffs along two dimensions: policies and income. Increased exactions in one may be compensated for by increased indulgences in another. Secondly, Hirschman looks only at one side of the bargain; as a result, he fails to analyze the potential for strategizing. In the context of the tax problem, for example, he analyzes the behavior of only the supplier of taxes; the behavior of the "demander" – the monarch – is ignored. But obviously both sides belong in the model; and knowing that the holders of taxable assets can exit, the demanders of taxes would surely take into account the potential for that behavior in calculating their best revenue strategy.

Both considerations come into play in generating the divergence between Hirschman's conclusions and our own. The capacity for strategic calculations by maximizing monarchs results in the owners of *mobile* factors, which the monarch seeks to tax, being compensated along the second dimension, that is, being given greater influence over the policy choices of governments. Surely in politics, even if not in markets, a model that incorporates strategic behavior is to be preferred.

---

[22] Albert O. Hirschman, 1970, *Exit, Voice and Loyalty: Response to Decline in Firms, Organizations, and States.* Cambridge: Harvard University Press.

CONCLUSION

The model depicts the relationship between economic actors and revenue-seeking governments and highlights factors that shape the manner in which those with power will choose to employ it.

In doing so, it suggests that as economies develop, those who preside over the state will exercise its power with greater restraint. They will become more "democratic." In countries whose economies are slower to develop, however, governments will tend to be authoritarian. Cross-national data confirm this implication of the model.[23]

---

23. See Seymour Martin Lipset, 1959, "Some Social Requisites of Democracy." *American Political Science Review* 53(1) (March), 69–105. For a skeptical review, see Daron Acemoglu, Simon Johnson, James Robinson, and Pierre Yased, 2008, "Income and Democracy." *American Economic Review* 208(3), 808–842.

APPENDIX TO CHAPTER 6

As described in the text, the problem may be written in the following form:

(i) Producers, given t and V, choose K and L to maximize

$$u^2\Big((1-t)f(K,L) - rK - wL, -(V-V^-)^2\Big).$$

The solution of this maximization problem can be characterized as

$$K^*(t,V), L^*(t,V).$$

(ii) Government, knowing $K^*(t, V)$ and $L^*(t, V)$, then chooses t and V to maximize

$$u^1\Big(tf(K^*,L^*), -(V-V^+)^2\Big).$$

Such that

$$u^2\Big((1-t)f(K^*,L^*) - rK^* - wL^*, -(V-V^-)^2\Big) \geq u^{-2}.$$

Before deriving the results, some assumptions are imposed:

$u_1^1 > 0, u_1^2 > 0, u_2^1 > 0, u_2^2 > 0$. Also, both u^1 and u^2
are quasi-concave functions.   (A1)

$f(K, L)$ is a quasi-concave function.   (A2)

$$max_{(K,L)}\, u^2\Big((1-t)f(K,L) - rK - wL, -(V^+-V^-)^2\Big)$$
$$< u^{-2}, \forall^- t \in [0,1]. \qquad\qquad\qquad\qquad\qquad\qquad (A3)$$

Now, the first order conditions for the producers' problem are:

$$(1-t)f_K = r, (1-t)f_L = w.$$

Therefore, the government's problem can be rewritten as:

$$\underset{(t,V,K,L)}{max}\; u^1\Big(tf(K,L), -(V-V^+)^2\Big) + \lambda_1[(1-t)f_K - r] + \lambda_2[(1-t)f_L - w]$$
$$+ \mu(u^2 - u^{-2}).$$

The first-order conditions, then, are:

$$u_1^1 f(K,L) - \lambda_1 f_K - \lambda_2 f_L + \mu[-f(KL)u_1^2] = 0 \qquad (1)$$

$$-2(V - V^+)u_2^1 + \mu u_2^2\left(-2(V - V^-)\right) = 0 \tag{2}$$

$$tu_1^1 f_K + \lambda_1(1 - t)f_{KK} + \lambda_2(1 - t)f_{KL} + \mu u_1^2[(1 - t)f_K - r] = 0 \tag{3}$$

$$tu_1^1 f_L + \lambda_1(1 - t)f_{KL} + \lambda_2(1 - t)f_{LL} + \mu u_1^2[(1 - t)f_L - w] = 0 \tag{4}$$

$$(1 - t)f_K = r \tag{5}$$

$$(1 - t)f_L = w \tag{6}$$

$$\mu(u^2 - u^{-2}) = 0, \mu \geq 0, u^2 \geq u^{-2} \tag{7}$$

Substitute equations (5) and (6) into equations (3) and (4), respectively. Then, by Cramer's rule, we can solve for λ_1 and λ_2 as follows:

$$\begin{bmatrix} \lambda_1 \\ \lambda_2 \end{bmatrix} = \frac{-u_1^a t}{(1 - t)(f_{KK}f_{LL} - f_{KL}^2)}\begin{bmatrix} f_K f_{LL} - f_L f_{KL} \\ -f_K f_{KL} + f_L f_{KK} \end{bmatrix}. \tag{8}$$

Substituting (8) into (1), after algebraic manipulations, we have

$$u_1^1\left[1 - \frac{t\eta}{1 - t}\right] = \mu u_1^2 \tag{9}$$

where η is the supply elasticity such that

$$\eta = \frac{-f_k^2 f_{LL} + 2f_K f_L f_{KL} - f_L^2 f_{KK}}{f(f_{KK}f_{LL} - f_{KL}^2)}. \tag{10}$$

Lemma 1. $t < \frac{1}{1+\eta}$.

Proof: By A1 and A3, we know $\mu \neq 0$, $u_1^1, u_1^2 > 0$. Hence equation (9) implies

$$1 - \frac{t\eta}{1 - t} > 0 \rightarrow t\eta < 1 - t \rightarrow t < \frac{1}{1 + \eta}.$$

Lemma 2. $\frac{\partial(V-V^-)}{\partial t} < 0$ along the optimal solutions path.

Proof: Since $\mu \neq 0$, hence along the optimal solutions path, $u^2 = u^{-2}$. By taking the total derivative, we thus have

$$-u_1^2 f(K, L)dt - 2(V - V^-)u_2^2 d(V - V^-) = 0$$

$$\rightarrow \quad \frac{\partial(V - V^-)}{\partial t} = \frac{-u_1^2 f(K, L)}{2(V - V^-)u_2^2} < 0.$$

To proceed further, two additional assumptions are imposed:

$$u^1(\cdot, \cdot) = tK^a L^\beta - log(V - V^+)^2 \text{where } a + \beta < 1. \tag{A4}$$

$$u^2(\cdot, \cdot) = (1 - t)[K^a L^\beta - rK - wL] - log(V - V^-)^2. \tag{A5}$$

Lemma 3. $\frac{\partial t}{\partial \eta} < 0.$
Proof: Under (A4) and (A5), the equation (9) is reduced to

$$1 - \frac{t\eta}{1 - t} = \mu. \tag{11}$$

On the other hand, equation (2) implies

$$-2(V - V^+)\frac{1}{(V - V^+)^2} + \mu[-2(V - V^-)]\frac{1}{(V - V^-)^2} = 0 \tag{12}$$

$$\rightarrow V - V^- = \frac{\mu}{1 + \mu}(V^+ - V^-) = \frac{1 - t - t\eta}{2 - 2t - t\eta}(V^+ - V^-), \text{by}(11).$$

Hence,

$$\frac{\partial(V - V^-)}{\partial t} = \frac{-\eta}{(2 - 2t - t\eta)^2}(V^+ - V^-). \tag{13}$$

Also, Lemma 2 claims

$$\frac{\partial(V - V^-)}{\partial t} = -\tfrac{1}{2}f(K, L)(V - V^-)$$
$$= -\tfrac{1}{2}f(K, L)\frac{1 - t - t\eta}{2 - 2t - t\eta}(V^+ - V^-). \tag{14}$$

Comparing equation (13) to equation (14), we have

$$\frac{\eta}{2 - 2t - t\eta} = \tfrac{1}{2}(1 - t - t\eta)f(K, L). \tag{15}$$

By taking the total derivative, we have

$$\left[\frac{\eta(2+\eta)}{(2-2t-t\eta)^2} + \frac{1}{2}(1+\eta)f(K,L)\right]dt = \left[-\frac{t}{2}f(K,L) - \frac{t\eta}{2}\frac{\partial f(K,L)}{\eta}\right.$$

$$\left.-\frac{2-2t}{(2-2t-t\eta)^2}\right]d\eta.$$

Hence, $\frac{\partial t}{\partial \eta} < 0$.

Lemma 4. At any fixed t, $\frac{\partial^2 (V-V^-)}{\partial t \partial \eta} < 0$.

Proof: By taking the partial derivative with respect to equation (13),

$$\frac{\partial^2(V-V^-)}{\partial t \partial \eta} = \frac{2-2t+t\eta}{-(2-2t-t\eta)^3}(V^+ - V^-) < 0.$$

7

The Political Impetus for the Great Transformation

INTRODUCTION

The study of development is the study of change. It is the study of the exodus of people from villages and farms to towns and cities, the rise of industry, the (relative) decline of agriculture, and the rise of average incomes. It is the study of the great transformation.[1]

To thus characterize development, however, is not to explain it. To explain it, we need to investigate the forces that animate these transformations and the behavior that generates such outcomes.

Both Marxists and development economists argue that the impetus for the great transformation came from the industrial sector, be it from the political power of the bourgeoisie or from the productive power of industrial technology. But upon closer examination, we find that much of the political impetus came from governments. Many governments followed mercantilist policies and promoted the fortunes of manufacturers and industrialists.[2] And while industry and manufacturing claim pride of place in today's industrialized economies, in many nations governments champion the interests of farmers. They protect local markets against imports of agricultural products; purchase the surpluses grown in response to the prices that result; and offer subsidies to those who grow

Excerpted from Robert Bates and William Rogerson, 1989, "Agriculture in Development: A Coalitional Analysis." *Public Choice* 39(5), 513–527.
[1] The phrase comes from the classic work, Karl Polyani, 1957, *The Great Transformation*. Boston: Beacon Press.
[2] See Eli F. Heckscher, 1955, *Merchantilism*. London: Allen and Unwin; D. Gale Johnson, 1973, *World Agriculture in Disarray*. New York: St. Martin's Press.

crops, raise livestock, or even refrain from farming.[3] Clearly, then, while sectors may dominate an economy, they may fail to dominate the polity; other political forces remain in play.

In this chapter, we address the political processes that transform economies and animate sectoral change. Doing so, we set out a model that, while based on individual farms and firms, generates political winners and losers at the sectoral level. At the core of the model stand "interests"– a political phenomenon more frequently studied in developed than in developing societies, but one that, judging by the results generated here, should feature more prominently in the development literature.[4]

AGRICULTURE IN DEVELOPMENT

In many developing nations, agriculture employs more people and generates more income than any other sector.[5] And yet, in the less-developed countries, public policy is often employed to shift relative prices against agriculture and in favor of industry and manufacturing.[6] Several explanations have been advanced to account for this bias. These explanations differ in character.

---

[3] Ibid.

[4] See the review by Mika Levaque-Manty, 2006, "Bentley, Truman and the Study of Groups." *Annual Review of Political Science* 9, 1–18.

[5] See Figures 1.1 and 1.2 in Chapter 1.

[6] As Raj Krishna writes in his important review paper: "As part of development policy, agricultural price policy has generally been used negatively – to keep bread and raw materials cheap for the growing industrial sector, and to maximize and to transfer to the city for investment the profits of trade in agricultural commodities." Raj Krishna, 1967, "Agricultural Price Policy and Economic Development," in Herman M. Southworth and Bruce F. Johnston, eds., *Agricultural Development and Economic Growth*. Ithaca: Cornell University Press, p. 498. See I. M. D. Little, T. Scitovsky, and M. Scott, 1970, *Trade and Industry in Some Developing Countries*. London: Oxford University Press, for an analysis of the impact of commercial policies on agriculture. For an impressionistic analysis of the impact of domestic policies, see Michael Lipton, 1977, *Why Poor People Stay Poor: Urban Bias in World Development*. Cambridge, MA: Harvard University Press. For a more rigorous treatment of the issues raised by Lipton, consult the technical papers of various World Bank and International Labor Organization reports; for example, see the technical papers for the International Bank for Reconstruction and Development, 1975, *Kenya: Into the Second Decade*. Baltimore and London: The Johns Hopkins University Press, or for the International Labor Organization, 1976, *United Nations Development Program, Growth, Employment and Equity: A Comprehensive Strategy for Sudan*. Geneva: International Labor Organization, United Nations Development Program. Or see such country studies as Doris Jensen Dodge, 1977, *Agricultural Policy and Performance in Zambia*. Berkeley, CA: Institute of International Studies.

One approach views the state as an agency for the maximization of social welfare; this is classically the view of the literature in development economics. Most commonly, economic growth is seen as a primary objective for poor societies. Based on empirical evidence and theoretical analysis, this approach argues that growth necessarily entails a shift of resources out of agriculture and into "more productive" sectors of the economy. The selection of policies to induce this shift via the manipulation of relative prices is seen as an appropriate choice, given the societies' objectives. There are numerous critics of this approach. But they often fail to challenge the basic assumption concerning the social welfare– maximizing basis for the selection of public policies.[7]

Other explanations do challenge this premise. Some can be classed as "sectoral models." These sectors are variously labeled as "urban" or "rural" or "modern" or "traditional"; sometimes intermediate sectors, labeled "informal" or "transitional," are included as well. The implication of this approach is that the policy bias in the developing areas represents the political domination of the "advanced" sector and its use of the instruments of the state to induce the transfer of resources from the more "backward" sectors of the society.[8]

Here I offer an alternative explanation for changes in the political position of agriculture as nations develop. I focus on interest groups.[9] According to the literature on interest groups, *particular* interests drive *public* policy. In particular, economic interests seek to shift relative prices to their advantage and do so by manipulating the state. Their ability to manipulate relative prices through public channels is determined by their ability to gain public support, that is, to form coalitions and gain backing from other interests for their demands. Within this framework, I try to deduce who would be the "winners" and who the "losers" and so

[7] See, for example, the contributions in Hollis Chenery, Montek S. Ahluwalia, C. L. G. Bell, John H. Duloy, and Richard Jolly, 1975, *Redistribution with Growth*. London: Oxford University Press.
[8] These models become variants of the first kind when they assume that all savings take place in the advanced sector or that there are discontinuous leaps between the production functions of the two sectors, that of the advanced sector yielding greater output per worker. With such assumptions, the rate of growth for the economy as a whole can be maximized by transferring resources to the advanced sector. For a review of much of this literature, see Dale W. Jorgenson, 1969, "The Role of Agriculture in Economic Development: Classical versus Neoclassical Models of Growth," in Clifton R. Wharton, Jr., ed., *Subsistence Agriculture and Economic Development*. Chicago: Aldine, pp. 320–348.
[9] The approach so pervades the literature on politics that it is impossible to point to definitive text.

characterize the group that would prevail in the use of the state to set relative prices to its advantage.

The model is based upon the assumption that the actors are both producers and consumers. Price rises achieved by one industrial group therefore have negative effects on the members of the group itself (insofar as producers of a good are also consumers of it); they also have negative effects on other groups. Consequently, *ceteris paribus*, any group seeking to maximize its real incomes by forming a coalition to secure a price rise has an incentive to exclude from that coalition industries whose goods comprise a high share of that group's purchases and to seek instead an alliance with industries whose goods constitute a lower share. In interpreting our results, it is important to note that food forms a relatively large part of the typical consumer's budget and that this is particularly the case in poor societies.

I demonstrate that in a simply stylized relative prices game, strong incentives exist for a winning coalition to form and characterize its size and composition: the winning coalition will consist of more than half but less than all of the industrial groups. The groups that are excluded from the winning coalition will consist of those whose goods comprise the highest share of a typical consumer's budget. Among them are farmers.

Lastly, I note the behavior of groups excluded from the winning coalition. At one extreme, these groups form one large counter coalition; this result represents total polarization of the political economy. At the other, they form a cascade of progressively smaller coalitions; extreme fragmentation prevails among the losers in the struggle for policies in support of shifts in relative prices. The likelihood of polarization tends to increase in economies where the winning coalition can secure larger income redistributions.

ASSUMPTIONS

Several assumptions underlie the model:

Concerning the Economy

That there are a number of different goods being produced in the economy. A good may be thought of as being very specific (such as flashlight batteries) or as being very general (such as food). The issue of what constitutes a good is central to the interpretation of our model and it will therefore be discussed further when elaborating our results.

That people specialize in production but generalize in consumption. That is, they earn their incomes from the production of a particular good and they spend their incomes broadly, allocating only a portion to the consumption of the good that they themselves produce and the remainder to the purchase of a wide variety of other goods.

That all people exhibit the same consumption pattern in the sense that all spend the same fraction of their incomes upon any given good. I also assume that the entire group of firms producing any given good – that is, an industry – acts as a single bargaining agent. Finally, I assume that the representative consumer exhibits unitary elasticity demand curves. We will speculate on the impact of relaxing these last three assumptions in the concluding section.

Concerning the Polity

I assume that the polity has control over policy instruments that can be used to manipulate relative prices. The government can do such things as impose tariffs upon imported goods that compete with domestic products, allow or aid in the exercise of monopoly power, regulate prices in certain industries, and so forth.

And that public policy measures are largely a response to the formation of pressure groups. In this connection, there are four additional assumptions:

i. That the magnitude of the price increases conferred depends on the coalitional structure exhibited by the industries seeking to influence public policy. In particular, in the political process represented in our model, size counts: the greater the number of industries in a petitioning coalition, the larger the price rise conferred by the state.

ii. That all industries have equal lobbying power in the sense that if two industries were to trade places in a given coalitional structure, they would receive each other's price rise.

iii. That all potential members of a given coalition act as if they expect to receive equal percentage price rises.

iv. And that a coalition's nominal price increase depends only on its own size and not on the size of competing coalitions.

The first assumption requires little comment. It simply reflects the centrality of interest group politics to the policy-making process and motivates interest group formation by rewarding the formation of coalitions. Which industries band together and the relative magnitude of the coalitions they form – that is the coalitional structure – determine the nature of the shift in relative prices generated by the public sector.

The second assumption lends clarity to the essential points of theorems and their proofs. This assumption is not necessary for the derivation of our formal results and the generalized versions of the theorems and proofs where appropriate. The concluding section discusses the implications of relaxing this assumption in the context of the problem addressed by this chapter.

Assumption iii requires that, in appraising coalitions, persons act as if they expect to be accepted as "equal partners." Such beliefs could derive from two sources. Most obviously, reality may in fact suggest that equity is a common occurrence; and there is some evidence to support this inference.[10] Second, actors attempting to make a complete assessment of their best strategies would have to gather huge amounts of information and make extremely complex calculations. They therefore have strong incentives to adopt simplified means of making probabilistic assessments of the relative desirability of various coalitions. One method would be to calculate the average or expected worth of a coalition; and one way of doing that would be to assume that any member would do no better or no worse than any other member.

The fourth assumption requires that the rise in prices secured by a given coalition not be affected by the behavior of industries excluded from that coalition. Because other coalitions are themselves seeking nominal price rises, the real incomes of the members of any particular coalition are of course affected by the behavior of persons outside of it; but the magnitude of the shifts in the prices of goods made by persons in the coalition are not.

Two justifications can be offered for this assumption. First, ignoring the possibility that industries may actively lobby against one another and reduce one another's nominal incomes can be viewed as a useful simplification; it enables us to isolate and secure unambiguous predictions about the effects of real price considerations in a relative prices game. Second, the assumption conforms in a natural way with the structure of the situation represented by the model and the kinds of behavior to which it would likely give rise. As it is assumed that each person earns all his

---

[10] E. E. Schattschneider, 1974, *Politics, Pressures and the Tariff*. New York: Arno Press, pp. 92ff. For another important study, see Jonathan Pincus, 1977, *Pressure Groups and Politics in Antebellum Tariffs*. New York: Columbia University Press.

income from the production of one commodity and spends it over many, the real incomes of the persons represented by the model are most directly affected by the price of the particular good that they produce rather than by the price of any particular good that they consume (and which is produced by others). In a world of limited resources with which to lobby, we might therefore expect persons to devote the bulk of their resources to lobbying for price increases for the goods they make. It should be noted that these expectations appear to be consistent with behavior in the real world. For example, Schattschneider, in his classic study of interest group behavior in the setting of United States' tariffs found that lobbying was most often "offensive" (i.e., in favor of changing the status quo), "primary" (i.e., engaged in by producers rather than consumers), and "positive" (i.e., in favor of increased tariffs). In particular, he documents "the desultory and fitful character of ... opposition" to petitions for increased rates.[11] And in our own interviews with the members of the Price and Income Board in Ghana we found that the Board acted in response to petitions for increased prices; the opposition it encountered, when it encountered any at all, took the form of demands for equalizing upward adjustments in the prices of other commodities.

Given these assumptions, we attempt to predict what coalitions will form and to determine the nature of the coalition whose interests will prevail in a political economy that exhibits the characteristics we have outlined.

THE MODEL

It is most natural to consider the economy as consisting of a finite number of industrial groups, $i = 1, \ldots, n$. Assume that there is a single owner of each industry. Let $(X_1^j, \ldots, X_n^j)$ be the goods bundle consumed by owner j. Let $(P_1, \ldots, P_n)$ be the price vector for the goods. Owner j derives his income from the sale of good j. His income, I_j, is thus

$$I_j = \sum_{i=1}^{n} X_1^i P_j. \tag{1}$$

Let α_i be the fraction of his income that each owner spends on good i; recall that we are assuming that this fraction is the same for each owner.

[11] Schattschneider, *Politics*, p. 109.

$$\alpha_i = \frac{PiX_i^j}{Ij} \text{ for any } j = 1, \ldots, n. \tag{2}$$

We will call owner i's share of the GNP, his real income, R_i

$$R_i = I_i f \sum_{j=1}^{n} I_j. \tag{3}$$

It is easy to see that, because of our symmetry assumptions about people's consumption habits, R_i equals α_i. Substitute (1) into (3) to yield

$$R_i = \left[\sum_{k=1}^{n} X_i^k P_i \right] f \left[\sum_{j=1}^{n} \sum_{k=1}^{n} X_j^k P_j \right]. \tag{4}$$

Now substitute (2) into (4).

$$R_i = \left[\sum_{k=1}^{n} \alpha_i J_k \right] f[\Sigma_{j=1}^{n} \Sigma_{k=1}^{n} \alpha_j I_k]. \tag{5}$$

Which simplifies to

$$R_i = \alpha_i / [\Sigma_{j=1}^{n} \alpha_j] = \alpha_i.$$

Now suppose that industry i receives a price rise of $(S_i - 1) \times 100$ percent. (An increase of 1.5 is an increase of $(1.5 - 1) \times 100$ – i.e., 50 percent.) Then by the same algebra as above the real income of owner i now becomes:

$$R_i = S_i \alpha_i f[\Sigma_{j=1}^{n} S_j \alpha_j] \tag{6}$$

It turns out to be mathematically more convenient to consider the economy as consisting of a continuum of industrial groups on the interval $(0, 1)$.[12] To translate to the continuous case let α and S be real valued continuous functions on $(0, 1)$. Assume that we have ordered the industrial groups in terms of increasing shares of the consumer's budget (i.e., $i < j$ implies $\alpha(i) < \alpha(j)$).[13] The "rule" for translating from sums to integrals is

[12] The consequent smoothness means that we are not troubled with boundary problems; in the discrete case, we would be. All that follows could be carried through in somewhat clumsier form for the discrete case.

[13] Actually, all proofs go through essentially unchanged with the weaker assumption that $\alpha(i) < \alpha(j)$. However, the proofs become more cumbersome, so we formally consider the simpler case.

$$\frac{1}{n}\Sigma_{j=1}^{n}\alpha_j = \int_0^1 \alpha_1 d_j. \tag{7}$$

Therefore the function α should have the property that

$$\int_0^1 \alpha_{(j)}d_j = \frac{1}{n}. \tag{8}$$

The real income of owner i, $R_{(i)}$, is now

$$R_{(i)} = \alpha_i / \left[n \int_0^1 \alpha_{(j)} d_j \right], \tag{9}$$

which, as in the discrete case, equals α_i. After each industry receives a price rise of $(S_{(i)} - 1) \times 100$ percent, the real income of owner i is

$$R_{(i)} = S_i\alpha_i / \left[n \int_0^1 S_{(j)}\alpha_{(j)} d_j \right]. \tag{10}$$

Price rises are generated by coalitions, and larger coalitions generate larger price rises. Call any Lebesgue measurable subset, C, of $(0, 1)$ whose measure is nonzero a coalition. Let the Lebesgue measure of the coalition, $\mu(C)$, be the measure of its size. Let f be the function from size of the coalition to the percentage price increase it generates. Assume that f is continuous and increasing. Then $f \bullet \mu(C)$ is the percentage increase in price generated by coalition C for its members.

A set of coalitions that are mutually disjoint and collectively exhaustive is then a complete description of the coalitional behavior of all economic agents in this model. We call such a set a coalition structure. Let C be a coalition structure and let $C_{(i)}$ be the coalition to which owner i belongs. Then the percentage increase in price that owner i receives is $f \bullet \mu \bullet C_{(i)}$. Substituting into (10), the real income of owner i under coalition structure C is

$$f \bullet \mu \bullet C_{(i)}\alpha_{(i)} / \left[n \int_0^1 f \bullet \mu \bullet C_{(j)} d_j \right]. \tag{11}$$

That is, once we know *C*, we can write out a real-valued function on (0, 1) that yields the real incomes achieved under *C* by all players. Let $\gamma(C)$ be this real valued function (i.e., γ is a function from coalition structures to real valued functions on (0, 1)).

The magnitudes of real payoffs are thus a function of the structure of the coalitions that form. Benefits derived from nominal increases in one's own price (as reflected in the numerator of (11)) must be adjusted for the loss in purchasing power resulting from increases in prices brought on by the operation of all coalitions (as reflected in the denominator of (11)). Under the circumstances, what coalitions will form? Can we predict how persons who derive their income from different commodities will group themselves and coalesce in the search for the most beneficial shift in prices?

THE EQUILIBRIUM COALITION

To answer this question, we assume that players desire to guarantee themselves the highest payoff possible. Let *g*(*C*) be the function that gives every member's evaluation of coalition *A*; *g*, that is, is a function from coalitions to real valued functions on the coalition). For $i \in A$ we have

$$[g(A)](i) = \inf\{[\gamma(C)](i) : A \in C\}. \tag{12}$$

The right-hand side of (12) simply gives the minimum real income that owner *i* could conceivably receive, given that coalition *A* formed with him as a member.

If we could identify a coalition such that every potential member could maximize the level of his guaranteed income by joining it, we could legitimately call such a coalition an equilibrium coalition. All of its potential members would view its formation as the best possible outcome of their search for partners with whom to petition for shifts in relative prices; within no other coalition could they do so well. They then have no reason to continue their search for partners.

The major results of this chapter are that an equilibrium coalition exists, all equilibrium coalitions are of the form[14] [0, *r*] where ½ < *r* < 1, and largest and smallest equilibrium coalitions exist. In particular, some

---

[14] As is the case for all coalitions, it is unimportant whether endpoints of segments are included or not. We will adopt the convention of including the right endpoint. Any set of measure zero can always be added or subtracted from a coalition without changing the results. Therefore "uniqueness" always is meant to be interpreted as uniqueness up to changes of measure zero.

industries will always be excluded from the equilibrium coalition. Furthermore, the excluded industries will always be those with the highest values of α (i.e., those whose goods comprise the highest share of representative consumers' budget).

Note as well that it is legitimate to call the equilibrium coalition "the winning coalition." Being over "½" in size and therefore the largest coalition, the equilibrium coalition receives the largest upward revision in relative prices. And by so doing, it achieves an increase in the real incomes of its members greater than that achieved by any other coalition. In effect, the equilibrium coalition is thus able to achieve changes in public policies whereby the interests of its members prevail; its members are able to secure policies that shift prices and thereby redistribute income from excluded persons to themselves.

Theorem 1:

  i. All equilibrium coalitions are of the form $[0, r]$ where $½ < r < 1$.
  ii. At least one equilibrium coalition exists.
  iii. There exists a smallest and a largest equilibrium coalition.

The proof of this theorem is contained in an appendix that is available from the authors upon request.[15]

EQUILIBRIUM COALITION STRUCTURE

The question now arises: how can we characterize equilibrium behavior for the economy as a whole that naturally incorporates the notion of the equilibrium coalition?

To address these questions we need two definitions.

Definition 1:
Let C be a subset of $[0, 1]$. Then C^* is a *constrained equilibrium coalition* in C if for every i in C^*, $(g. (\cdot)) (i)$ is maximized by C^* over the set of coalitions that are subsets of C.
Definition 2:
Let C be a coalition structure. Then C is an *equilibrium coalition structure* if C has at most a countable number of elements and they can be ordered $C = \{C_i\}_{i=1}^{n}$ (where n may be ∞) such that for every $i = 1, \ldots, n$, C_i is a constrained equilibrium coalition in $\{\cup C_i\}(j = 1, \ldots, n)$.

---

[15] It is best to contact William Rogerson at the Department of Economics, Northwestern University.

The following theorem establishes that such an equilibrium exists and is of a particularly natural form.

Theorem 2:

At least one equilibrium coalition structure exists. All equilibrium coalition structures are of the form

$$\{[0, r_1](r_1, r_2](r_2, r_3]...(r_n, 1]\}.$$

Or

$$\{[0, r_1](r_1, r_2](r_2, r_3]...\}.$$

Furthermore, letting $r_0 = 0$, $(1 + r_{i-1})/2 \leq r_i \leq 1$ for $i = 1, 2, \ldots$, something that follows immediately from Lemma 9.[16]

It is difficult to identify interesting parameters that affect the number of coalitions in the equilibrium structure in a predictable manner. However, loosely speaking, the larger the income of the agents in the winning coalition, the fewer will be the number of coalitions forming among the excluded agents.

To see this, note that, mathematically, the search for a constrained equilibrium coalition in $(r, 1]$ amounts to a search for the value of s in $(r, 1]$ which maximizes

$$\frac{f(s)}{\delta + f(s)[A(r+s) - A(r)] + f()1 - r - s}.$$

The constrained equilibrium coalition is then $(r, s]$. The number δ is the nominal income of the agents in $[0, r]$. For example if they are in a single coalition, then δ is $f(r)A(r)$. Rewrite this as

$$\frac{f(s)}{\delta + \Gamma(s)}.$$

Then, at an internal maximum,

$$\frac{f'(s)}{f(s)} = \frac{\Gamma'(s)}{\delta + \Gamma(s)}.$$

It is easy to show that in the implicit function thus defined, $ds/d\delta > 0$. That is, all interior local maximums move to the right when income of agents in $[0, r]$ becomes larger. It is also easy to show that if δ is small enough, then the

---

[16] Once again, it is best to contact William Rogerson at the Department of Economics, Northwestern University.

global maximum is definitely interior; and that if δ is large enough, then the global maximum is at $s = 1$. These results suggest that, *ceteris paribus*, we are likely to see a larger number of coalitions in equilibrium if the shape of f and A is such as to generate smaller incomes for agents in the winning coalition.

CONCLUSION

In interpreting these results, we can make use of several characteristics of the economies of the developing nations. The first is that consumers in poor nations spend a very large portion of their incomes on food – in many cases, in excess of 50–60 percent. The second is that specialization in the developing economies appears to have proceeded much further in the "modern sector" – that is in manufacturing – than it has in agriculture. Thus, in the manufacturing sector, there are firms that specialize in the production of such items as clothing, bicycles, soap, and toothpaste; but in agriculture, "firms" often amount to peasant farmers who grow a full range of crops with which to meet their subsistence needs and who simply market their surplus production. In other words, agricultural producers supply "food" as opposed to "wheat," "lettuce," "tomatoes," or what not.

In terms of our model, these considerations imply that agricultural producers can be assigned very high "a's." In the process of coalition formation, they therefore constitute relatively unattractive partners; for, should they be granted a price rise, this would be very costly to all other members of the coalition. Persons seeking to influence the state so as to secure higher real incomes therefore have a strong incentive to exclude agricultural producers from the policy determining coalitions in preference to other partners who possess lower "a's."

Under such circumstances, our model suggests, an equilibrium coalition should exist and food producers are unlikely to be members of it. Such a coalition would maximize the level of the guaranteed income of all prospective members; it would represent the best possible outcome of their search for lobbying partners, and there are therefore strong incentives for it to form. Moreover, our model suggests that such a coalition would be composed of persons who draw their incomes from the production of goods characterized by the lower range of "a's," i.e., by "a's" that are of a magnitude more typically exhibited by manufactured goods than by food.

Thus far, we have confined our attention to the implications of our analysis for the status of agriculture within the political economies of the poor nations. But our model also gives insight into the changes that can take place in the status of this industry as nations develop. The two factors we used to identify the food-producing sector as a "high α" sector vanish when we consider the more developed economies. Food production becomes more specialized; rather than producing "food," farmers produce particular food items. As incomes rise, we observe progressively smaller fractions of income being spent on food. And the result of both changes is to lower the α's and thus to render agricultural producers more viable partners in coalitions seeking changes in relative prices.

One example of such a transformation is provided by Grant McConnell.[17] McConnell interprets the history of the American farm movement as a move from a relatively undifferentiated populist movement, largely excluded from the benefits of the policy-making process, to a highly differentiated set of commodity groups, each ensconced within a highly privileged, crop specific, public-policy program. We interpret this transformation as exhibiting the expected correlates of a change in the location of agriculture in the equilibrium solution to a relative prices game.

More generally, the underdeveloped countries, which are overwhelmingly agricultural in composition, currently adopt policies that are antithetical to the immediate economic interests of the vast majority of their farmers. But rich nations, such as those in Europe and the United States, where agricultural producers constitute but a small fraction of the citizenry, frequently adopt public policies that shift relative prices in favor of food producers. This pattern has been one of the paradoxical features of the position of agriculture in the political economy of nations. Our model gives us insight into why something that appears so anomalous should instead be expected to exist.

Obviously, there are many other factors at work, many of which may have been excluded by our assumptions. Upon reflection however, relaxing some of these assumptions might actually tend to strengthen our conclusions.

Suppose, for example, we allowed variations in the elasticity of demand. Then an industry with a relatively higher elasticity of demand would be a more desirable partner, *ceteris paribus*, because a rise in its price would induce a smaller decline in real incomes. Consideration of this factor suggests that had we incorporated variable elasticities of demand our conclusions would rest on stronger grounds, for food consumption is highly price-inelastic. The relatively low elasticity of demand for food should therefore make food producers relatively less attractive as coalitional partners.

By assuming one firm per industry, we have also ignored the problems of political organization *within* industries. Note that a prime determinant of the relative ability of groups to form is their size. Size

[17] Grant McConnell, 1966, *Private Power and American Democracy.* New York: Knopf.

increases the costs of coordination, the perceived benefits of "free riding," and the costs of detecting such behavior. In most developing nations, the number of firms in the manufacturing sector is simply orders of magnitude fewer than the number of "firms" in agriculture. Being more numerous, agricultural producers might well face higher costs and perceive fewer individual benefits from organizing. They might therefore be more likely to find themselves excluded.

We assumed that the size of a shift in relative prices obtained by a coalition was a function only of the size of the coalition; in particular, it was not a function of who was in it, and the admission of one more industry yielded the same increase in price irrespective of which industry it was. If we relax this assumption, then *ceteris paribus*, industries that are less able to secure price rises than others are more likely to be excluded from the winning coalition. Agriculture is likely to have a lower than average effect for at least two reasons. First, its greater difficulty of organizing, as discussed, might make it a less effective lobbyist than other groups. Second, in poorer nations, industrialization is widely held to represent the road to modernity; and as a consequence, most governments in the developing areas are more solicitous of the interests of industrial and manufacturing firms than they are of the interests of farmers. For both reasons, relaxing this assumption leads us to give even greater credence to the likelihood of agriculture's exclusion from the winning coalition.

Lastly, we have assumed uniform consumption patterns among all economic interests. Engel's law operates within as well as between societies, however, and the owners of urban industries will of course not spend as high a proportion of their incomes on food as will their employees. It is our contention, however, that they will nonetheless negotiate as if they had the same consumption patterns as had the poorer workers. For incomes of owners are derived from the profits of their firms; and their profits are vulnerable to claims by the workers for adjustments to compensate for an erosion in their real incomes. These claims can be made either through the use of a competitive labor market or through recourse to strike action. In either case, the real income of the owners will be influenced far more by changes in the price of goods consumed by the workers than by changes in the price of the goods that the owners themselves consume. Given the state of the literature in this field, it is therefore ironic and informative that our analysis underscores the role of *lower class* interests in building coalitions in the political economies of the developing nations.

Considering the effects of factors that we have excluded from the model thus leaves us optimistic concerning the robustness of our results.

8

Shaping the Path of Growth and Development

The developing world is characterized not only by low average incomes but also by high levels of economic instability. The variation in growth rates "is great, relative to ... the average level," to quote Lant Pritchett, and volatility, however defined, "is ... much greater in developing than in industrial countries."[1] So too is the level of political conflict.[2] In this, the concluding chapter, we seek to link the politics to the economics of the developing world and to do so by tracing the links between political instability, political risk, and economic performance

In doing so, we make use of the standard model of a two-sector economy (e.g. Lewis, 1954), in which development results from the movement of resources from the less productive "informal" or "traditional" to the "formal" or "modern" sector of the economy.[3] Modern firms are

Jean Paul Azam, Robert Bates, and Bruno Biais, 2009, "Political Predation and Economic Development." *Economics and Politics* 22(3), 255–277. Transforming the original article into a chapter for a book led to the rewriting of portions of the text. These alterations in no way alter the arguments originally advanced.

[1] Lant Pritchett, 2000, "Understanding Patterns of Economic Growth." *World Bank Economic Review* 14, 221–250, at 221.

[2] See, for example, Christopher Blattman and Edward Miguel, "Civil War," NBER Working Paper 14801 March 2009; and D. Rodrik, 1999, "Where Did All the Growth Go? External Shocks, Social Conflict, and Growth Collapses." *Journal of International Economics* 40, 1–22.

[3] A. Lewis, 1954, "Economic Development with Unlimited Supplies of Labor." *Manchester School of Economic and Social Studies* 22, 139–191. Note, however, that our model does not explicitly rely on economies of scale, and thus differs from the class of two-sector models running from P. Rosenstein-Rodan, 1943, "Problems of Industrialization in Eastern and South-Eastern Europe." *Economic Journal* 53, 202–211; to M. Murphy, A. Shleifer, and R. Vishny, 1989, "Industrialization and the Big Push." *Journal of*

more productive, we assume, but also more visible and therefore more vulnerable to political predation. Informal activities are less visible, and it is more costly and less rewarding for the government to expropriate them.[4] When polities turn predatory, then, they often target the formal sector – the most productive sector of the national economy.

Each period, citizens choose whether to operate in the informal or formal sector. Then the government, if opportunistic, decides whether to predate. The government's choice provides a signal of its type.[5] While predation generates immediate benefits, restraint enhances political optimism, encouraging citizens to enter the formal sector. An opportunistic government, rationally anticipating the response of the citizens, trades off the immediate costs of restraint against the benefits of future predation. Its strategy takes the form of mixing between predation and restraint. The a priori distribution of the government's type and of its policy choices determine the citizens' assessment of political risk and thus the growth of the economy.[6]

As long as the government does not predate, political optimism increases; as resources flow to the modern sector, the economy expands. Citizens, however, realize that predatory governments might well mimic the behavior of benevolent ones. They are not certain whether the history of restraint reveals the presence of a benevolent government or merely reflects the efforts of a predatory one to "fatten" the modern sector before engaging in predation. The resulting increase in political risk lowers the growth rate. It also shapes the distribution of income. Because wages in the modern sector can be expropriated, they include a risk premium.

The model thus generates patterns that are consistent with recent empirical findings: persistent divergences,[7] sustained growth often

Political Economy 97, 1003–1026; and M. Murphy, A. Shleifer, and R. Vishny, 1989, "Income Distribution, Market Size and Industrialization." *Quarterly Journal of Economics* 104, 537–564.

[4] H. de Soto, 1989, *The Other Path*. New York: Harper & Row.

[5] Our analysis is in line with the reputation models of D. Kreps and R. Wilson, 1982, "Reputation and Imperfect Information." *Journal of Economic Theory* 27, 253–279; and P. Milgrom and K. Roberts, 1982, "Predation, Reputation and Entry Deterrence." *Journal of Economic Theory* 27, 280–312.

[6] Thus policy risk arises endogenously, reflecting the strategies of political and economic agents. This differs from exogenous random policy reversals or changes in the government (A. Alesina and G. Tabellini, 1989, "External Debt, Capital flight and Political Risk." *Journal of International Economics* 27, 199–220; D. Rodrik, 1991, "Policy Uncertainty and Private Investment in Developing Countries." *Journal of Development Economics* 36, 229–243).

[7] A. Maddison, 2001, *The World Economy: A Millennial Perspective*. Paris: Development Center of the OECD.

followed by economic collapse,[8] regime shifts that follow a Markov process,[9] and political events that trigger these changes.[10]

---

[8] W. Easterly, M. Kremer, L. Pritchett, and L. Summers, 1993, "Good Policy or Good Luck? Country Growth Performance and Temporary Shocks." *Journal of Monetary Economics* 32, 459–483; Pritchett, "Understanding Patterns of Economic Growth."

[9] M. Jerzmanowski, 2006, "Empirics of Hills, Plateaus, Mountains, and Plains: A Markov-Switching Approach to Growth." *Journal of Development Economics* 81, 357–385.

[10] R. Hausmann, F. Rodriguez, and R. Wagner, 2006, *Growth Collapses*. Cambridge, MA: Center for International Development, Harvard University; D. Rodrik, 1999, "Where Did All the Growth Go? External Shocks, Social Conflict, and Growth Collapses." *Journal of International Economics* 40, 1–22.

Our theoretical analysis also generates dynamics that are in line with the empirical findings of E. Glaeser, R. La Porta, F. Lopez de Silanes, and A. Shleifer, 2004, "Do Institutions Cause Growth?" *Journal of Economic Growth* 9, 271–303. In our equilibrium as well as in their empirical results, poor countries get out of poverty when dictators follow good policies and during this process, institutions improve. Our chapter complements the institutionalist theories of development (see, e.g., D. Acemoglu and S. Johnson, 2004, "Unbundling Institutions." MIT Department of Economics Working Paper No. 03–29; D. Acemoglu, S. Johnson, and J. A. Robinson, 2001, "The Colonial Origins of Comparative Development: An Empirical Investigation." *American Economic Review* 91, 1369–1401; D. Acemoglu, S. Johnson, and J. A. Robinson, 2002, "Reversal of Fortune: Geography and Institutions in the Making of the Modern World Income Distribution." *Quarterly Journal of Economics* 117, 1231–1294; S. Engerman and K. Sokoloff, 1997, "Factor Endowments, Institutions, and Different Paths of Development among New World Economies," in S. Haber, ed., *How Latin America Fell Behind*. Palo Alto, CA: Stanford University Press; D. C. North and B. R. Weingast, 1989, "Constitutions and Commitment: The Evolutions of Institutions Governing Public Choice in Seventeenth-Century England." *Journal of Economic History* 69 (4), 803–832; H. Root, 1989, "Tying the King's Hands: Credible Commitments and Royal fiscal Policy during the Old Regime." *Rationality and Society* 1, 240–258.

In addition to institutions, we emphasize citizens' beliefs and heterogeneity in government types. Our approach is consistent with the empirical findings of Jones and Olken that leaders' identities matter for growth: B. F. Jones and B. Olken, 2004, "Do Leaders Matter? National Leadership and Growth since World War II." Working Paper, Northwestern University. It is also related to T. Besley, 1997, "Monopsony and Time-Consistency: Sustainable Pricing Policies for Perennial Crops." *Review of Development Economics* 1, 57–70. But, in the latter, in contrast with our analysis, there are no informational asymmetries about the type of the government, nor does predation occur on the equilibrium path. Our analysis also complements previous analyses of asymmetric information about governments. D. Rodrik, 1989, "Promises, Promises: Credible Policy Reform via Signaling." *Economic Journal* 99, 756–772, argues that good governments signal their types by implementing larger reforms than is first best. E. Perotti, 1995, "Credible Privatization." *American Economic Review* 85, 847–859, shows how benevolent governments breed confidence by following gradual privatization policies. See C. Phelan, 2004, "Public Trust and Government Betrayal." *Journal of Economic Theory* 127, 27–43 for a study of financial and monetary crises. Our modeling framework differs from Phelan's in particular because, unlike us, he assumes that there are unobservable changes in government type, and because we study wages and inequality, while he does not.

THE MODEL

Citizens and Government

Consider a discrete-time, infinite-horizon model where time t goes from 1 to infinity. The actors – each rational and risk neutral – include a unit mass continuum of private citizens and an agent that possesses the power to engage in predation. Before the game, nature selects the government's type. With probability π_0, the government is relatively benevolent. With the complementary probability $(1 - \pi_0)$, it is opportunistic.

We first assume that the benevolent government fully refrains from predation, while the opportunistic government must choose between full restraint and full predation. We later extend our analysis to consider a less stylized model and demonstrate that our qualitative results still obtain.

The Modern Sector and the Traditional Sector

We assume a two-sector economy. The traditional sector is less productive than the modern (which we also term the formal). Firms operating in the modern sector are more productive and development occurs as resources move from the traditional sector to the modern.

Denote by β_t the fraction of agents operating in the modern sector at time t, and by $1 - \beta_t$ the fraction of agents operating in the traditional sector. For simplicity, we set output in the traditional sector to $1 - \beta_t$, (i.e., the marginal product in the traditional sector is constant and normalized to 1). Output in the modern sector is $Y(\beta_t)$. The production function $Y(\cdot)$ is continuous, increasing, and concave. Again for simplicity, we consider only one input: labor.

We assume the modern sector is more productive than the traditional sector, that is, $Y'(\beta) \geq 1, \forall \beta \in [0, 1]$. To simplify the analysis we also assume that $Y'(1) = 1$, which implies that, when all agents work in the modern sector, marginal productivity is equalized in the two sectors. As will be seen, this assumption also implies that, with positive levels of political risk, the optimal value of β remains strictly lower than 1.

In this context, the first best allocation is the solution of $Max_{\beta_t \in [0,1]} Y(\beta_t) + (1 - \beta_t)$. Concavity of the production function implies that the second-order condition holds. Under our assumption that $Y'(1) = 1$, the optimum is pinned down by the first-order condition and

$\beta = 1$. When there is no risk of predation, the competitive equilibrium implements this allocation. Citizens working in the traditional sector obtain their marginal productivity equal to 1. Those employed in the modern sector receive wage w. As long as $\beta < 1$, equilibrium requires that workers be indifferent between taking a job in the modern sector and being self-employed in the traditional sector, implying that $w = 1$.[11] The modern sector firms are competitive and maximize profits $Y'(\beta_t) = \beta_t w$ taking wages as given. This yields the first best allocation.

The Risk of Predation

The greater efficiency of the formal sector comes at the cost of greater political risk. Whether because the firms are larger, less mobile, or more visible, an opportunistic government finds it not only more lucrative but also less costly to prey upon the formal sector. To capture this vulnerability in the simplest possible way, we initially assume that, when the government chooses to predate at time t, it endeavors to capture the output of the modern sector, $Y(\beta_t)$. If it is successful, the profits of private firms are entirely expropriated and wages in the modern sector are not paid. In contrast, we assume that output in the traditional sector is protected from political predation. Thus, the risk of political predation can deter citizens from leaving the safe traditional sector to enter the more productive modern sector.

At the beginning of each period, citizens make the initial move, choosing whether to work in the traditional or modern sector. The government then chooses whether to seize the output of the latter sector or to refrain from predation. Its strategy is described by the probability that it refrains from predation at time t, denoted by μ_t. If the opportunistic government never predates at time t, then $\mu_t = 1$. If it always engages in predation, $\mu_t = 0$.

The intermediary case ($0 < \mu_t < 1$) corresponds to a mixed strategy. Figure 8.1 portrays the sequence of play.

Predatory agents possess an incentive to pool with benevolent ones, initially refraining from predation so as to enhance their reputation and subsequently secure a larger gain.

Political Instability

The government's discount rate is $\delta_G < 1$, which can also be interpreted as the probability that the government remains in power. The two

---

[11] This indifference condition is sufficient but not necessary when $\beta = 1$.

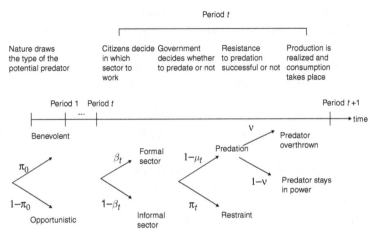

FIGURE 8.1 The sequence of play

interpretations – one in terms of discount rate and the other in terms of exogenous political shocks – are equivalent.

After predation, with probability v, the government is overthrown and a new government takes over, with initial reputation π_0. In that case, the modern sector is not expropriated and wages are paid. In contrast, when a government predates and stays in power, modern firms are expropriated and modern sector wages are not paid. To simplify the analysis, we assume $v < 1/Y'(0)$, which implies that when citizens are sure that the government will predate they prefer not to enter the modern sector.

The Dynamics: Equilibrium Divergence and Unstable Growth

In equilibrium, the dynamics of the political and economic variables can be modeled as a discrete Markov chain, with $T + 2$ states. The underlying state variable is the number of periods without predation, or, equivalently, the updated probability that the current government is benevolent. Correspondingly, we label the states by the tenure of the non-predatory government. In state 1, it is the first period during which the government is in office, either because the game is just starting or because the previous government has been overthrown and a new one has just been drawn. Similarly, in state 2 the government currently in place was new last period and did not predate then. In state 0, the government has already been observed to predate and has not been overthrown. More precisely,

- In *state* 0, the government is known to be predatory. Accordingly no citizen dares to enter the politically vulnerable modern sector. Hence, $\beta = Y = 0$.
- In *state* 1, the probability that the government is benevolent is π_0 and the fraction of the population working in the modern sector is $\beta_1 = B(\lambda_1)$.
- *State* $t \in \{2, \ldots, T\}$ arises after the government has been observed to show restraint during $t - 1$ periods. In that case, the probability that the government is benevolent is π_{t-1} and the fraction of the population working in the modern sector is $\beta_t = B(\lambda_t)$.
- *State* $T + 1$ arises after the government has been observed to show restraint during T periods. In that case, the government is known to be benevolent, and full development obtains, with $\beta_{T+1} = 1$.

The analysis in the appendix, and in particular Proposition 2, yields the transition probabilities that attach to each state. Interpreting δ_G as the probability that there is no exogenous political shock, we obtain the following:

Once the economy reaches state 0, it is trapped there until the government is overthrown because of an exogenous event. After such a shock (which happens with probability $1 - \delta_G$), the economy moves to state 1.

From state $t \in \{1, \ldots, T\}$, if there is an exogenous political shock, the economy enters state 1. Otherwise, if the government shows restraint, the economy moves to state $t + 1$. This transition, corresponding to gradual economic development, occurs with probability $\delta_G \lambda_t$. But if the government is observed to predate, the economy collapses. If the predatory government is overthrown, the economy moves to state 1, where it gets a fresh start. This sequence of events happens with probability $\delta_G(1 - \lambda_t)v$. If the predatory government stays in power, the collapse is durable, as the economy moves to state 0. This sequence of events happens with probability $\delta_G(1 - \lambda_t)(1 - v)$.

Once the economy reaches state $T + 1$, full development obtains. Full development persists with probability δ_G. If there is an exogenous political shock, which happens with probability $1 - \delta_G$, the economy moves back to state 1.

The dynamics of this Markov chain are illustrated in Figure 8.2. As the figure illustrates, the Markov chain is irreducible, that is, starting from any of the states it is possible to get to any of the other states. It is also aperiodic. It therefore admits a unique ergodic distribution. The transition probability matrix, which we denote by M, is

$$M = \begin{pmatrix} \delta_G & 1-\delta_G & 0 & 0 & \cdot & \cdot & 0 \\ \delta_G(1-\lambda_1)(1-v) & (1-\delta_G)+\delta_G(1-\lambda_1)v & \delta_G\lambda_1 & 0 & \cdot & \cdot & 0 \\ \vdots & \vdots & & \vdots & \cdot & \cdot & \vdots \\ \delta_G(1-\lambda_t)(1-v) & (1-\delta_G)+\delta_G(1-\lambda_1)v & 0 & \cdot & \delta_G\lambda_t & \cdot & 0 \\ \vdots & \vdots & & \vdots & \cdot & \cdot & \vdots \\ \delta_G(1-\lambda_T)(1-v) & (1-\delta_G)+\delta_G(1-\lambda_1)v & 0 & \cdot & \cdot & \cdot & \delta_G\lambda_T \\ 0 & 1-\delta_G & 0 & \cdot & \cdot & \cdot & \delta_G \end{pmatrix}. \quad (6)$$

The ergodic distribution is the probability vector P such that $MP = P$. It is given in the next proposition.

Proposition. In the ergodic distribution, the $T + 2$ possible states of the economy have equal weight.

The proposition implies that most of the time (T periods out of $T + 2$), the agents in the economy are unsure about the exact type of the government. The government has not been observed to predate and thus some fraction $\beta_t \in (0, \beta^*)$ of the agents choose to operate in the modern sector. $1/(T+2)$ of the time, however, the government is known to be predatory, and no one dares to enter the politically vulnerable sector. Also, $1/(T+2)$ of the time, the government is known to be benevolent, and the economy has reached full development.

Discussion

We close by noting several implications of the analysis. As will be noted, researchers have already confirmed several; the others provide opportunities for further testing.

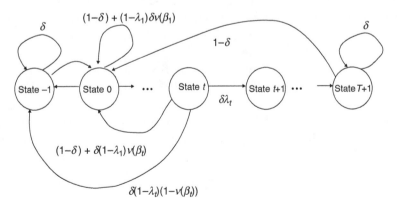

FIGURE 8.2 The equilibrium Markov chain.

Implication 1. Our model offers a theoretical rationale for the patterns observed by Pritchett[12]: Some countries have a steady growth path resembling "hills." In other countries, initial growth is followed by economic decline, a path resembling "mountains." In our model, "hills" arise in equilibrium when there is no predation and moderate but steady growth occurs. "Mountains" arise when the government eventually predates and growth collapses.

Our analysis suggests as well that:

Implication 2. The decline in growth rate associated with "mountains" should occur around the time of political predation and be large. The positive growth rates observed in the case of "hills" should be relatively smaller and follow political restraint.

Consider, for example, the case of Zimbabwe. Despite having endorsed socialist doctrines and overthrown the government of the prosperous European minority, so long as Mugabe ruled with restraint, Zimbabwe's economy grew. But when in 2002, Mugabe's supporters began to invade commercial farms and his colleagues to seize commercial and financial institutions, expectations radically altered. Investment ceased, capital and labor fled the formal economy, and Zimbabwe's once prosperous economy collapsed.

If Zimbabwe offers an example of a "mountain," Botswana stands as one of Pritchett's hills. At the time of independence, Botswana was poor; with a semi-arid economy and no known mineral wealth, the export of meat and hides underpinned its economy. While the subsequent discovery of diamond deposits offered the opportunity for growth, it also offered opportunity for predation. The deposits were located within the home district of the president, Seretse Khama, but he insisted that rights to the resources be vested in the nation. In addition, he recruited an economic team that devised policies aimed at maximizing the intertemporal flow of revenues from the deposits rather than their immediate consumption. Repeatedly signaling his role as a custodian of the wealth of the nation, Khama behaved with restraint. Our analysis implies that such restraint should have resulted in the expansion of the economy, and the data are consistent with such an implication.

---

[12] Pritchett, "Understanding Patterns of Economic Growth."

Implication 3. Consider the random variable taking the value 1 when predation occurs (which happens with probability $1 - \lambda_t$) and 0 otherwise. Its variance, $\sigma_t^2 = \lambda_t(1 - \lambda_t)$, is a measure of risk in our model. In the early stages of development, as the economy grows, both λ_t and σ_t^2 increase on the no-predation path. Once $\lambda_t > \frac{1}{2}$, which corresponds to a more mature economy, growth occurs while risk declines.

Implication 4. This reasoning implies that the level of political risk should trace a hump-shaped path. Other things being equal, political risk should be limited in poor stagnating economies, larger in developing economies, and low in developed economies.

When political risk is large, employees must be promised a relatively high wage in the case where the government does not predate and governments must promise high yields on their bonds.

Implication 5. Political risk generates a wedge between the wages promised in the modern sector and the traditional or informal sector and also increases the promised yield on government bonds. The greater the risk of predation, the larger these premia. The longer the period without predation, the lower these premia.

Starting with Simon Kuznets,[13] scholars have argued that inequality increases at initial stages of growth and then subsequently declines. This pattern is implied by the logic of the model. To quantify income inequality in our model, consider the Lorenz curve plotting the cumulative percentage of income against the cumulative percentage of population. The Gini coefficient is the area between the first diagonal and the Lorenz curve. In our model, this is

$$G = \frac{1}{2}\frac{(1-\beta)\beta(w-1)}{1+\beta(w-1)},$$

a function that is first increasing, and then decreasing in β. Hence, along the no-predation path, the Gini coefficient increases and then decreases, conforming to the logic of the Kuznets curve. Initially all workers operate in the traditional sector and there is no inequality. Then, as long as the government continues not to predate, workers progressively move to the modern sector where they earn larger wages. This induces an increase in inequality. If the government does not predate, the majority of the

---

[13] S. Kuznets, 1955, "Economic Growth and Income Inequality." *The American Economic Review* 45(1), 1–28.

population eventually moves to the modern sector and inequality decreases. And if the government predates, the population reverts to the traditional sector, where inequality is low.

In a country with little political risk and an initially reputable government, the initial rise in inequality should be limited and income inequality quickly diminish. With large predation risk, the initial increase in inequality is stronger, since the political premium in wages is greater, and it takes longer for a reduction in inequality to obtain. Thus, our model yields a sixth empirical implication:

Implication 6. Countries with greater initial political risk should have more humped Kuznets curves.

The ability to extract a fraction of the output via taxation reduces the temptation for opportunistic governments to engage in full predation. In practice, it is difficult for governments to extract resources from the private sector and θ is constrained to be small when taxation institutions are weak, which is typical of poor countries. This leads to our next implication.

Implication 7. Weak taxation institutions enhance political risk.

In addition to the inefficiency of the fiscal system, international pressure can constrain the ability of governments to extract resources from the private sector. Developed nations can curb aid or raise tariffs when governments do not follow internationally approved "best practices." In our model, this leads to a decrease in θ. Rich and powerful countries can also inflict punishments when governments exert full predation, which, in our model, increases v.

The late twentieth century offers an example. During the Cold War, the ability of the developed democracies to punish misbehaving rulers in the South was limited by the need for allies in the struggle against communism. With the fall of the Soviet Union, Western democracies had less need for allies and were therefore more willing to pressure governments in the developing world to limit predatory practices. The surge in political instability associated with the end of the Cold War is consistent with this implication of our model.

What of governments who have spoiled their reputations? Are their nations fated to remain poor? Our model offers the following, rather pessimistic implication:

Implication 8. When they engage in full predation, governments ruin their reputation and are afterwards unable to recover them. In such cases, growth will return only after major political changes, as when new regimes assume power.

This implication of our theoretical analysis is consistent with the findings of Haggard and Webb and Jones and Olken.[14]

Theoretical models such as this give greater reason to focus on the *political* economy of development. Our work should thereby strengthen the hand of those seeking to empirically investigate the impact of politics on the economic performance of nations.

---

[14] S. Haggard and S. B. Webb, eds., 1994, *Voting for Reform*. New York: Oxford University Press for the World Bank; Jones and Olken, "Do Leaders Matter?"

APPENDIX I TO CHAPTER 8

EQUILIBRIUM HISTORIES

The joint evolution of predation and entry in the formal sector arises as the equilibrium outcome of a dynamic game. At each point in time, t, the private sector and the government choose their optimal actions: β_t and μ_t. Denote by π_{t-1} the updated probability that the government is non-predatory, given the sequence of moves from time 1 to time $t-1$.

The state variable is the reputation of the government, π_{t-1}, or equivalently the number of periods during which this government has shown restraint. Markov-perfect equilibrium requires that each agent takes optimal actions, given its rational interpretation of past observations, summarized by π_{t-1}, and its rational anticipations about the optimal actions taken in the continuation subgames.[15]

The Dynamics of Political Risk

Denote by λ_t the probability that the government will show restraint at time t given the information set of the agents in the economy:

$$\lambda_t = \pi_{t-1} + (1 - \pi_{t-1})\mu_t. \tag{1}$$

Applying Bayes' rule, the dynamics of π_{t-1} as a function of μ_t and the sequence of moves is readily obtained, and is given in the next lemma.

Lemma 1. As soon as the government predates, π_{t-1} goes to 0. If the government has not predated at time $1, ..., t-1$, the probability that it is benevolent is

$$\pi_{t-1} = \frac{\pi_0}{\pi_0 + (1 - \pi_0)\mu_1 ... \mu_{t-1}}.$$

Lemma 1 implies that, on the no-predation path, the probability that the government is benevolent increases, that is, the reputation of the government improves over time. On the other hand, when the government predates, its reputation is permanently destroyed.

---

[15] E. Maskin and J. Tirole, 2001, "Markov Perfect Equilibrium, I: Observable Actions." *Journal of Economic Theory* 100, 191–219.

Private Sector Choices

Citizens who choose to operate in the traditional sector receive their marginal product, equal to 1. Those who choose to operate in the modern sector at time t receive their wage w_t if the government continues not to predate or if, after attempting to predate, the government is overthrown. Equilibrium in the labor market implies that citizens be indifferent between self-employment in the informal sector and employment in the modern sector. Hence,

$$w_t = \frac{1}{\lambda_t + (1 - \lambda_t)c}. \qquad (2)$$

Taking the wage rate as given, the modern sector firms choose how many workers to hire to maximize expected profits:

$$\max_{\beta_t \in [0,1]} \left(\lambda_t + (1 - \lambda_t)v\right)\left(Y(\beta_t) - \beta_t w_t\right).$$

Substituting in the equilibrium wage, expected profits in the modern sector are $\left(\lambda_t + (1 - \lambda_t)v\right)Y(\beta_t) - \beta_t$. The solution of this program is given in the next lemma.

Lemma 2. If $\lambda_t = 1$, then all citizens operate in the modern sector. If $\lambda_t = 0$, then all citizens operate in the traditional sector. For interior values of λ_t, the fraction of citizens employed in the traditional sector, β_t, is an increasing function of λ_t denoted by $B(.)$:

$$\beta_t = B(\lambda_t) = Y'^{-1}\left(\frac{1}{\lambda_t + (1 - \lambda_t)v}\right). \qquad (3)$$

As the probability that there will be no predation (λ_t) rises from 0 to 1, the fraction of the population working in the formal sector $[B(\lambda_t)]$ increases from 0 to 1. Since the modern sector is more productive than the traditional one, GDP per capita is increasing in λ_t, (i.e., it is decreasing in political risk). Note also that the sensitivity of economic development (β_t) to political risk (λ_t) is lower when the ability of the people to resist full predation (v) is large.

For interior values of β, the fraction of the population operating in the formal sector is given by the first-order condition:

$$Y'(\beta_t) = w_t = \frac{1}{\lambda_t + (1 - \lambda_t)v},$$

which simply equates the marginal productivity of labor to wages in the modern sector. The greater the political risk, the greater the wages necessary to attract agents in the modern sector.

The Program of an Opportunistic Government

We now analyze the problem from the point of view of an opportunistic government. Once the government has predated, its reputation is ruined; citizens permanently exit the vulnerable modern sector and there is no further predatory gain. Denote by J_t the value function of the opportunistic government if it has not predated until time t. The expected utility of the government when it engages in predation is the product of the probability that the government will stay in power and the output it can then ex-propriate. Denote this expected gain by $\varphi(\beta_t)$:

$$\phi(\beta_t) = (1 - v)Y(\beta_t).$$

Denote by J_t the value function of the opportunistic government after t periods of restraint. It is defined by the following Bellman equation:

$$J_t = \max_{\mu_t \in [0,1]} \{(1 - \mu_t)\phi(\beta_t) + \mu_t \delta_G J_{t+1}\}.$$

As long as the opportunistic government shows some restraint, that is, as long as $\mu_t > 0$, the first-order condition states that the government is indifferent between immediate predation and restraint.[16] Thus, on the no-predation path, $\phi(\beta_t) = (1 - v)Y(\beta_t)$. This equality emphasizes the link between the value function of the government and the current level of development of the modern sector. Indeed, the latter determines how much the government can obtain if it predates immediately, thus anchoring its value function.

Equilibrium

From this infinite-horizon game, a finite horizon emerges endogenously. Intuitively, as the number of periods without predation increases, the updated probability that the government is benevolent increases. This increased optimism generates an increase in the fraction of the population operating in the formal sector. The expansion of the modern economy, in

---

[16] $\mu_t = 1$ never arises in equilibrium. Were citizens to expect $\mu_t = 1$, then restraint at time t, while costly for the impatient government, would not improve its reputation.

turn, raises the attractiveness of predation for the opportunistic government. At some point, the temptation grows so large that an opportunistic
government can no longer resist. At this point, it predates.

To make this point more formally, first define β^* as the level of development of the formal sector such that the opportunistic government is
indifferent between predating now and waiting, for full development at
the next period:[17]

$$\beta^* = Y^{-1}\left(\delta_G Y(1)\right).$$

Second, define π^* as the level of the probability that the government is
benevolent, such that a fraction β^* of the citizens is willing to enter the
modern sector, even while anticipating that the government, if opportunistic, would predate for sure, that is, $\beta^* = B(\pi^*)$. Since B is increasing it is
invertible. Hence we can write π^* as

$$\pi^* = B^{-1}(\beta^*).$$

The following proposition directly stems from these definitions.

Proposition 1. When π_t reaches π^*, then the following is a Nash equilibrium of the continuation game: an opportunistic government
always predates ($\mu_t = 0$) and a fraction β^* of the citizens choose to
enter the formal sector. If there is no predation at time t, then the
economy reaches full development at the next period, that is
$\beta_{t+s} = 1, \forall s \geq 1$.

Denote by T the endogenous horizon of our politico-economic game.
After observing $T - 1$ periods without predation, the probability that the
government is benevolent reaches π^*.[18] Thus, at time T, by construction,
the value function of the government is $J_T = \delta_G \phi(1)$. Before time T, the
government follows a mixed strategy and thus is indifferent between
predation and restraint. Hence, $J_{T-1} = \phi(\beta_{T-1}) = \delta_G^2 \phi(1)$. Iterating,
$J_{T-k} = \phi(\beta_{T-k}) = \delta_G^{k+1} \phi(1)$. As noted in the following lemma, this expression pins down the value function of the opportunistic government and

---

[17] Note that β^* is strictly lower than 1.
[18] Because we work in discrete time, we face an integer number problem: at time $T - 1$, the
conditional probability that the government is opportunistic is strictly below π^*, and at
time T it is (generically) strictly above. To avoid technicalities, we neglect the integer
problem, and work as if at time T the updated probability that the government is
opportunistic just reached π^*.

the fraction of the population operating in the modern sector on the no-predation path.

Lemma 3. On the no-predation path, $\forall t \leq T$, the opportunistic government value function is

$$J_t = \delta_G^{T+1-t} \phi(1), \tag{4}$$

and the fraction of the population working in the modern sector is

$$\beta_t = \phi^{-1}\left(\delta_G^{T+1-t} \phi(1)\right). \tag{5}$$

The mixed strategy indifference condition implies that the value function of the opportunistic government on the no-predation path is the present value of its payoff at the endogenous final date T, as stated in equation (4). This value function increases with time. The indifference condition also implies that the fraction of the population operating in the modern sector is $\phi^{-1}(J_t)$. Since $\phi(\cdot)$ is increasing between 0 and β^*, β_t also increases with time on the no-predation path.

Turning to the dynamics of political risk, equation (3) expresses the fraction of the population operating in the modern sector in a given period as a function of the probability that there will be no predation during that period. Since this function is increasing, it can be inverted, which yields $\lambda_t = B^{-1}(\beta_t)$. Substituting the equilibrium fraction of the population employed in the modern sector from equation (5), we obtain the following lemma:

Lemma 4. After $t-1$ periods without predation, the citizens evaluate the probability of no current predation as

$$\lambda_t = B^{-1}\left(\phi^{-1}\left(\delta_G^{T+1-t} \phi(1)\right)\right) = B^{-1}\left(Y^{-1}\left(\delta_G^{T+1-t} Y(1)\right)\right),$$

which is increasing in t.

Summarizing these results, on the no-predation path the modern sector gradually increases in size. So too does per capita income and the ability of the civil society to resist expropriation. During this process, political risk decreases. Our theoretical analysis thus offers an equilibrium interpretation for the jointly endogenous evolution of the economy and the polity. But, even with successful development, in equilibrium, as long as $t < T + 1$, predation can occur.

To complete the characterization of equilibrium strategies, we need to determine the strategy of the opportunistic government and the citizens' beliefs (i.e., the evolution of μ_t and π_{t-1}, on the no-predation path). This can be achieved by drawing upon the implications of Bayes' rule for the dynamics of beliefs (Lemma 1), and combining the analysis of private sector choices (Lemma 2) with that of the government strategy (Lemmas 3 and 4).

Proposition 2. There exists an equilibrium whereby after a sufficiently long time without predation the updated probability that the government is benevolent reaches π^*. On the no-predation path, the equilibrium probability that the opportunistic government refrains from predation is

$$\mu_t = \frac{\lambda_1 \ldots \lambda_t - \pi_0}{\lambda_1 \ldots \lambda_{t-1} - \pi_0} = \frac{\prod_{s=1}^{t} B^{-1}\left(\phi^{-1}\left(\delta_G^{T+1-s}\phi(1)\right)\right) - \pi_0}{\prod_{s=1}^{t-1} B^{-1}\left(\phi^{-1}\left(\delta_G^{T+1-s}\phi(1)\right)\right) - \pi_0},$$

$$\forall t > 1 \text{ and } \mu_1 = \frac{\lambda_1 - \pi_0}{1 - \pi_0},$$

While the equilibrium probability that the government is benevolent is

$$\pi_{t-1} = \frac{\pi_0}{\lambda_1 \ldots \lambda_{t-1}} = \frac{\pi_0}{\prod_{s=1}^{t-1} B^{-1}\left(\phi^{-1}\left(\delta_G^{T+1-s}\phi(1)\right)\right)}, \forall t > 1.$$

APPENDIX 2 TO CHAPTER 8

Proof of Lemma 2. β_t is chosen to maximize $\left(\lambda_t + (1 - \lambda_t)v\right)Y(\beta_t) - \beta_t$. When $\lambda_t = 1$, the optimum is $\beta_t = 1$ and when $\lambda_t = 0$ it is $\beta_t = 0$. Turning to interior values of λ_t, first note that the derivative of the objective function with respect to β_t is $\left(\lambda_t + (1 - \lambda_t)v\right)Y'(\beta_t) - 1$. The second-order condition holds since the production function is concave. The constraints $\beta_t \leq 1$ and $\beta_t \geq 0$ are not binding. Hence, the optimum is pinned down by the first-order condition, that is,

$$Y'(\beta_t) = \frac{1}{\lambda_t + (1 - \lambda_t)v}. \tag{A1}$$

The right-hand side of (A1) is decreasing in λ_t, while its left-hand side is independent of λ_t. Hence, an increase in λ_t implies an increase in the value of β_t for which the two curves intersect. $\square$

Proof of Proposition 1. By definition, when π_{t-1} reaches π^* and a fraction β^* of the citizens enter the formal sector. Since they anticipate that the opportunistic government always predates at this point in time, after observing no predation at time t, the citizens rationally update π_t to 1. Hence, if the opportunistic government waits another period before predating, his expected utility is $\delta_G\varphi(1)$. Consequently, by construction of β^*, predating now is optimal for the opportunistic government. $\square$

Proof of Proposition 2. The proof proceeds in three steps:

First step: Relying on Lemma 1, (1), and Bayes' law, we obtain μ_t and π_{t-1} as a function of λ_t. The probability of restraint at time 1 is $\lambda_1 = \pi_0 + (1 - \pi_0)\mu_1$. This implies that $\mu_1 = (\lambda_1 - \pi_0)(1 - \pi_0)^{-1}$. The proof proceeds by induction.

To prove that the property holds at time 2, we must prove that $\mu_2 = (\lambda_1\lambda_2 - \pi_0)/(\lambda_1 - \pi_0)$. The probability of restraint at time 2 is $\lambda_2 = \pi_1 + (1 - \pi_1)\mu_2$. Thus, $\mu_2 = (\lambda_2 - \pi_1)(1 - \pi_1)^{-1}$. From Lemma 1, $\pi_1 = \pi_0(\pi_0 + (1 - \pi_0)\mu_1)^{-1}$. Hence,

$$\mu_2 = \frac{\lambda_2[\pi_0 + (1 - \pi_0)\mu_1] - \pi_0}{(1 - \pi_0)\mu_1}.$$

Substituting in $\lambda_1 = \pi_0 + (1 - \pi_0)\mu_1$ and $(1 - \pi_0)\mu_1 = \lambda_1 - \pi_0$, $\mu_2 = (\lambda_2\lambda_1 - \pi_0)(\lambda_1 - \pi_0)^{-1}$, completes the first step of the proof. Next we need to prove that if the property holds until time $t - 1$, then it also holds at time t. By definition of $\lambda_t, \mu_t(\lambda_t - \pi_{t-1})(1 - \pi_{t-1})^{-1}$. From Lemma 1,

$$1 - \pi_{t-1} = \frac{(1 - \pi_0)\mu_1...\mu_t}{\pi_0 + (1 - \pi_0)\mu_1...\mu_t}.$$

Substituting in μ_t,

$$\mu_t = \frac{\lambda_t[\pi_0 + (1 - \pi_0)\mu_1...\mu_{t-1}] - \pi_0}{(1 - \pi_0)\mu_1...\mu_{t-1}}.$$

That the property holds for all time $\tau < t$ implies that

$$\mu_1...\mu_{t-1} = \frac{\lambda_1 - \pi_0}{1 - \pi_0}\frac{\lambda_1\lambda_2 - \pi_0}{\lambda_1 - \pi_0}...\frac{(\lambda_1...\lambda_{t-1}) - \pi_0}{(\lambda_1...\lambda_{t-2}) - \pi_0}$$

$$= \frac{(\lambda_1...\lambda_{t-1}) - \pi_0}{1 - \pi_0}.$$

Substituting $\mu_1 ... \mu_{t-1}$ into μ_t, the result obtains. Finally turn to the analysis of π_{t-1}. As shown above in this proof,

$$\mu_1...\mu_{t-1} = \frac{(\lambda_1...\lambda_{t-1}) - \pi_0}{1 - \pi_0}.$$

Substituting $\mu_1 ... \mu_{t-1}$ into π_{t-1}, we get $\pi_{t-1} = \pi_0/(\lambda_1...\lambda_{t-1})$.

Second Step: Relying on the first step we prove that there exists a time T at which π_{t-1} reaches π^*. Since λ is increasing in t,

$$\pi_{t-1} = \frac{\pi_0}{\lambda_1...\lambda_{t-1}} > \frac{\pi_0}{(\lambda_{t-1})^{t-1}} > \frac{\pi_0}{(\lambda_T)^{t-1}} = \frac{\pi_0}{(\pi^*)^{t-1}}.$$

Since π^* is a constant lower than 1, as t goes to infinity, $\pi_0/[(\pi^*)^{t-1}]$ grows unboundedly. Hence, there exists a value of t such that π_{t-1} reaches π^*.

Third step: Combining Lemma 4, which gives λ_t as a function of the exogenous parameters, and the previous step of the proof, which gives μ_t and π_{t-1} as functions of λ_t, we obtain the strategy of the opportunistic government and the beliefs of the citizens. Substituting in the value of β_t from Lemma 3, we obtain the value of λ_t stated in the proposition. Substituting $\pi_{t-1} = \pi_0/(\lambda_1 \dots \lambda_{t-1})$ in the value of λ_t given above, we obtain

$$\pi_{t-1} = \frac{\pi_0}{\lambda_1 \dots \lambda_{t-1}} = \frac{\pi_0}{\prod_{s=1}^{t-1} B^{-1}\left(\phi^{-1}\left(\delta_G^{T+1-t}\phi(1)\right)\right)}.$$

Finally, substituting the value of λ_t into the value of μ_t given above, we obtain

$$\mu_t = \frac{(\lambda_1 \dots \lambda_t) - \pi_0}{(\lambda_1 \dots \lambda_{t-1}) - \pi_0} = \frac{\prod_{s=1}^{t} B^{-1}\left(\phi^{-1}\left(\delta_G^{T+1-t}\phi(1)\right)\right) - \pi_0}{\prod_{s=1}^{t-1} B^{-1}\left(\phi^{-1}\left(\delta_G^{T+1-t}\phi(1)\right)\right) - \pi_0}.$$

Proof of Proposition 3. The column vector P has $T + 2$ elements, denoted by p_i, $i \in \{0, 1, \dots, T+1\}$. Multiplying the first row of M by P, we obtain $p_0\delta_G + p_1(1 - \delta_G)$, which simplifies to $p_0 = p_1$. Multiplying the second row of M by P, we obtain

$$p_0\delta_G(1 - \lambda_1)(1 - v) + p_1\left((1 - \delta_G) + \delta_G(1 - \lambda_1)v\right) + p_2\delta_G\lambda_1 = p_2.$$

Substituting $p_0 = p_1$ and simplifying, we obtain $p_0 = p_2$. Iterating, we find that all the elements of P are equal. □

$$\pi_{t-1} = \frac{\pi_0}{\lambda_1 \dots \lambda_{t-1}} = \frac{\pi_0}{\prod_{s=1}^{t-1} B^{-1}\left(\phi^{-1}\left(\delta_G^{T+1-t}\phi(1)\right)\right)}.$$

Proof of Proposition 3. The column vector P has $T + 2$ elements, denoted by p_i, $i \in \{0, 1, \dots, T+1\}$. Multiplying the first row of M by P, we obtain $p_0\delta_G + p_1(1 - \delta_G)$, which simplifies to $p_0 = p_1$. Multiplying the second row of M by P, we obtain

$$p_0\delta_G(1 - \lambda_1)(1 - v) + p_1\left((1 - \delta_G) + \delta_G(1 - \lambda_1)v\right) + p_2\delta_G\lambda_1 = p_2.$$

Substituting $p_0 = p_1$ and simplifying, we obtain $p_0 = p_2$. Iterating, we find that all the elements of P are equal.

9

Conclusion

The developing countries emerged from the detritus of war. Politically and economically depleted, European states freed their colonies and the developing nations were born. That this is so renders it surprising that so few who study development appear to recognize or to acknowledge the importance of politics. While many focus on the policies governments choose and pursue, fewer probe the reasons that impel them to do so.

Much of the literature on development is therefore "welfarist" in tone and content. It ignores the political games that shape the choices governments make and the trade-offs, bargains, and betrayals that generate the outcomes that follow. Many write as if describing the distribution of food baskets to the poor in nineteenth century Europe. They ignore the role of politics and its significance for development.

A major goal of this book has been to reframe the manner in which development is viewed by those who study it. It has been to place politics at the center of development studies.

While pursuing this objective, I have analyzed politics as if it were a game. I have done so not to trivialize its significance; I fully realize that as a result of how political games are played, lives are altered, saved, and lost. Rather I do so in order to gain sharper and deeper insights into how governments behave. Applying game theory allows me to place the study of the political economy of development on "micro-foundations." It enables me not only to describe and to probe but also to explain. It leads, that is, to Q.E.D – *quid erat demonstrandum* – a rare resting place for those who study development.

Index

Roger Schoenman, *Networks and Institutions in Europe's Emerging Markets*

Lyle Scruggs, *Sustaining Abundance: Environmental Performance in Industrial Democracies*

Jefferey M. Sellers, *Governing from Below: Urban Regions and the Global Economy*

Yossi Shain and Juan Linz, eds., *Interim Governments and Democratic Transitions*

Beverly Silver, *Forces of Labor: Workers' Movements and Globalization since 1870*

Prerna Singh, *How Solidarity Works for Welfare: Subnationalism and Social Development in India*

Theda Skocpol, *Social Revolutions in the Modern World*

Austin Smith et al, *Selected Works of Michael Wallerstein*

Regina Smyth, *Candidate Strategies and Electoral Competition in the Russian Federation: Democracy Without Foundation*

Richard Snyder, *Politics after Neoliberalism: Reregulation in Mexico*

David Stark and László Bruszt, *Postsocialist Pathways: Transforming Politics and Property in East Central Europe*

Sven Steinmo, *The Evolution of Modern States: Sweden, Japan, and the United States*

Sven Steinmo, Kathleen Thelen, and Frank Longstreth, eds., *Structuring Politics: Historical Institutionalism in Comparative Analysis*

Susan C. Stokes, *Mandates and Democracy: Neoliberalism by Surprise in Latin America*

Susan C. Stokes, ed., *Public Support for Market Reforms in New Democracies*

Susan C. Stokes, Thad Dunning, Marcelo Nazareno, and Valeria Brusco, *Brokers, Voters, and Clientelism: The Puzzle of Distributive Politics*

Milan W. Svolik, *The Politics of Authoritarian Rule*

Duane Swank, *Global Capital, Political Institutions, and Policy Change in Developed Welfare States*

David Szakonyi *Politics for Profit: Business, Elections, and Policymaking in Russia*

Sidney Tarrow, *Power in Movement: Social Movements and Contentious Politics*

Sidney Tarrow, *Power in Movement: Social Movements and Contentious Politics, Revised and Updated Third Edition*

Tariq Thachil, *Elite Parties, Poor Voters: How Social Services Win Votes in India*

Kathleen Thelen, *How Institutions Evolve: The Political Economy of Skills in Germany, Britain, the United States, and Japan*

Kathleen Thelen, *Varieties of Liberalization and the New Politics of Social Solidarity*

Charles Tilly, *Trust and Rule*

Daniel Treisman, *The Architecture of Government: Rethinking Political Decentralization*

Guillermo Trejo, *Popular Movements in Autocracies: Religion, Repression, and Indigenous Collective Action in Mexico*

Guillermo Trejo and Sandra Ley, *Votes, Drugs, and Violence: The Political Logic of Criminal Wars in Mexico*

CPSIA information can be obtained
at www.ICGtesting.com
Printed in the USA
LVHW031711060221
678577LV00001B/70

9 781108 930932